PRAISE FOR

Conflict Sparks Change

"Over the years, I've been very impressed watching Kim Fair-cloth and Dawn Bedlivy develop highly practical and effective approaches for helping individuals and teams manage workplace conflict. In *Conflict Sparks Change: 8 Field-Tested Strategies for Human Resources Professionals,* they share their insights and offer helpful strategies, tips, reflective questions, and processes for addressing inevitable conflicts. HR professionals will treasure this new offering from Faircloth and Bedlivy."

—**CRAIG RUNDE,** co-author of *Becoming a Conflict Competent Leader* and *Building Conflict Competent Teams*

"In *Conflict Sparks Change*, authors Kim Faircloth and Dawn Bedlivy offer a fresh and insightful perspective tailored to modern human resources professionals. They explore the evolving expectations placed on senior leaders and supervisors to be mindful of their influence on the workforce, particularly in setting the tone for conflict resolution. The book provides real-world examples highlighting the increasing importance of HR's collaboration with in-house counsel, emphasizing that this partnership is not only valuable but essential. A central theme is that conflict, when properly managed, can be a catalyst for positive change, and embracing it is critical for fostering innovation."

—**DIANE M. JANOSEK,** executive director, Capitol Technology University's Center for Women in Cyber

8

Field-Tested Strategies for Human Resources Professionals

CONFLICT SPARKS CHANGE

KIM FAIRCLOTH, PHD
& DAWN BEDLIVY, ESQ

RIVER GROVE
BOOKS

Published by River Grove Books
Austin, TX
www.rivergrovebooks.com

Distributed by River Grove Books

Design and composition by Greenleaf Book Group
Cover design by Greenleaf Book Group
Cover images used under license from ©Adobestock.com

Publisher's Cataloging-in-Publication data is available.

Print ISBN: 978-1-63299-921-4

eBook ISBN: 978-1-63299-922-1

First Edition

To my beloved husband, Kim, whose unwavering support and love has been my constant source of strength and inspiration. To my wonderful children, Matt, Megan, and Austin, who fill my life with joy, laughter, and endless motivation. To my family, whose encouragement and belief in me have been the foundation of my journey. To Buttons, my cherished pup and steadfast writing partner, whose quiet support filled every moment of this book with joy. And to all the dedicated human resources professionals, whose tireless efforts and commitment to fostering positive work environments make a difference every day. I love you all.

—Kim

To my children, Veronica, John, Patrick, and Katie, your light, passion, and young wisdom have been my guide and source of inspiration. To my mentors, friends, and coaches, your unwavering support and advice have enabled me to birth new ideas and share them with the world. To the community of ADR practitioners, and to all who seek to walk the path of peace, I hope this book serves as both a guide and reminder that the world needs what we have to offer.

—Dawn

And to God, who sent us lighted feet to follow, granting us the strength and wisdom to follow where he leads.

—Kim and Dawn

Contents

Authors' Note

Is it just us, or does it seem like the workforce is addicted to drama? As fellow human resources (HR) professionals, are you also spending way too much time on resolving employee relations matters and worrying about the opportunity cost of all this nonproductive conflict? Are you hiring for diverse perspectives and finding that the inability to have constructive debates about diverse ideas is causing business problems? If, like us, you're a bit overwhelmed and need field-tested conflict engagement tips, or if you just want to level up on the work required to deal with workplace conflict, this book of specific strategies is for you.

And if you happen to work in a drama-free environment, give yourself a reality check: there might just be smoke in your backyard that you're not checking into. HR aims to create an open environment where employees promptly address conflicts by visiting the HR office. This allows HR to stay informed about organizational issues and helps employees resolve concerns before they escalate. What we are more curious and concerned about are the simmering voices we don't hear—because as HR professionals, we know that workplace conflict impacts innovation and our workplace culture.

Some of you may be coming to this book frustrated, burned out, or pessimistic. Our challenge to you is this: try to read this book with a beginner's mindset by reaching way back to your desire to work in human resources. People are generally good, and sometimes people are a mess. You became an HR professional because you were drawn to working with people issues. When conflicts arise, you might actually get pretty pumped to put all that wisdom and training you've gathered to good use. In this post-pandemic world, employees and leaders are looking to you for your skills and know-how more than ever. It's a chance to show off what you've got! You picked this book up for a reason, and that tells us you are ready to explore conflict with a different mindset. We hope that you see this book as a personal professional growth handbook, and we hope you see us as a member of your community of practice because we are exactly that—HR professionals.

As two workplace alternative dispute resolution professionals with a combined 50-plus-year career in human resources and administrative law, we've been in the trenches and we get you. We have worked with and learned from your fellow HR professionals in for-profit, nonprofit, academic, and government settings. Like you, these HR professionals understand this foundational truth: if two or more people are working together, conflict exists. We know we can't avoid it; we have a lot of practice engaged in conflict, yet leading through conflict is still one of the most difficult and important human resources competencies. Your best employees do not want to work in organizations that won't deal with conflict. HR specialists help create cultures that celebrate constructive debate about diverse thoughts—but are also decisive when enough is enough. We want you to think of this book as mentoring on the topic of conflict by providing you with a series of strategies based on what we've learned.

Like you, our professional careers are grounded in a whole lot of theory and research, and business leaders want you to have that foundational competence and confidence. We also think that leaders want business partners with expertise on how to help them move from just managing conflict to steps for channeling specific business problems into better paths. Regardless of your job title (HR generalist, mid-level manager, supervisor, HR project leader), if you are responsible for guiding people through disagreements or differing ideas, you are managing conflict situations. This is a normal and expected part of leadership, and not something to be viewed negatively.

Given that reality, here's an analogy we'd like you to consider. When your computer acts up, you have some basic computer skills that allow you to deal with occasional blips. If that doesn't work, you might have to call a computer tech specialist. You are that same type of expert for human resources issues. When you speak with that computer expert, you aren't looking for a discussion on how to write software. You want specific, step-by-step help—and quickly. This is what your leaders want from you, and this book gives you plenty of on-the-job, results-oriented models to get you started.

In the upcoming chapters, we're sharing practical strategies that have been tried and tested in the field by us. These are the very same techniques we've shared with HR professionals and leaders during private coaching sessions focused on conflict resolution. These eight strategies can be considered your go-to handbook for improving your skills in handling conflicts, or simply increasing your chances of achieving positive outcomes in tough situations. There are no promises here of easy or flawless results; mastering workplace conflict is no simple feat. Let's face it: navigating conflicts in HR is a constant challenge. Humans are intricate beings, and every conflict scenario is unique. So approach this book as your own personal self-development "dojo" or practitioner's guide, providing you with both strategy and purpose as you strive to handle conflicts effectively and channel negative energy into more constructive avenues, thus reducing the negative impact of conflict drama.

While this book proves general guidance and advice on conflict resolution and restorative conversation practices, it is important to note that the power of an expert HR professional lies in their ability to customize this advice for the culture and specific needs of their employees or clients. The information presented here will help you create processes that are consistent, transparent, and tailored to your specific organizational needs. (It should not be considered a substitute for legal advice in complying with relevant laws and regulations.)

At the end of each chapter, you'll find critical thinking questions to prompt reflection and application. We encourage you to take these strategies and tailor them to fit your unique organizational context. What resonates with your experiences? What doesn't quite align, and how would you approach it differently? Whether you're just beginning to navigate conflicts or you have some of your own field-tested strategies, you're at a pivotal stage in your HR journey where journaling and self-reflection, coupled with actionable steps, will propel your growth. Remember, you are your own best self-development coach.

So fasten your seatbelt, because this book is brimming with innovative approaches to tackling the challenging terrain of workplace conflict. Let's embark on the journey of harnessing workplace conflict together!

The HR Professional's Role in Conflict

For HR professionals to effectively utilize the strategies outlined in this book, it is imperative that they possess a comprehensive understanding of the intricate dynamics of conflict. Conflict, far from being a simple interaction, is a complex interplay of various factors. It encompasses not only cognitive processes within the brain but also hormonal influences, deeply ingrained learned behaviors, and the contextual nuances of each specific moment.

To navigate conflict adeptly and stay present during very complex conversations, HR professionals must delve into the multifaceted nature of its origins and manifestations. The human brain contains cognitive biases and emotional responses that intertwine to shape our reactions to conflict situations. Hormonal fluctuations, which can be very difficult to manage, can significantly impact our perceptions and behaviors during conflict, further complicating the resolution process. Understanding the complex interplay of various factors encompassing cognitive processes, hormonal influences, learned behaviors, and contextual nuances is vital for HR professionals so that they can tailor conflict resolution strategies to specific situations.

Understanding the Dynamics of Conflict

Conflicts are not isolated incidents, and are often influenced by our past experiences and learned behaviors. Our individual backgrounds, cultural influences, and personal histories all contribute to how we engage with conflict and approach its resolution. Understanding these underlying patterns is essential for HR professionals seeking to address conflicts effectively within their organizational settings. The context in which a conflict arises plays a pivotal role in shaping its dynamics. Organizational culture, power dynamics, and external pressures—these factors and more exert influence on how conflicts unfold and escalate in the workplace. HR professionals must be attuned to these contextual nuances to tailor their conflict resolution strategies accordingly.

By grasping the complexities of conflict at both a psychological and contextual level, HR professionals can better equip themselves to implement the strategies delineated in this book and foster harmonious and productive workplaces. Here are a few of those underpinnings affecting conflict:[1]

---

1   Lisa Feldman Barrett, *How Emotions Are Made: The Secret Life of the Brain* (Boston: Houghton Mifflin Harcourt, 2017).

1. *Aggressive brain.* Our brain's emotion center (amygdala) and its control center (prefrontal cortex) team up to decide how we react in a conflict. If these areas aren't playing nice or if our brain chemicals are out of whack, we might be more likely to get aggressive.

2. *Hormone rollercoaster.* Hormones like cortisol (the surge hormone) can make us feel feisty or frazzled during a conflict. They're like the fuel that powers our reactions.

3. *Our genes/DNA.* Our genes give us our own unique temperament, which affects how we handle conflicts. Some of us might be more chill, while others are quick to blow up. It's all in our DNA.

4. *Our thoughts.* How we see things (perception), what we think about them (interpretation), and who we blame (attribution) can mess with how conflicts play out. We're all biased, which can turn small issues into big blowouts.

5. *Our basic survival instincts.* Back in the caveman days, conflict was often about who got the best food or mate. Those instincts are still lurking in our brains, pushing us to fight for what we want even if it's not life or death anymore.

6. *Family, friends, and society.* Our upbringing, culture, and environment all shape how we handle conflicts. If we grew up in a violent home or a competitive society, it can affect how we deal with disagreements.

All of this means that we must, as HR professionals, be the ones in the room (hopefully among others) who fundamentally believe that even with all of the above at play, change is possible. While we will encounter employees who seem to be stuck in a loop of aggression, with the right help and support, we can help them become more peaceful. If we recognize that our brains are constantly evolving, we know that this includes how we perceive conflict.

In addition, here's your new reality: the COVID-19 pandemic has made a huge impact on social norms and interpersonal reactions—some good and some very bad. The strategies in this book take this into account and update strategies we might have used as HR professionals in a comparatively stable and less fearful world.

For example, one current response to conflict is apathy. While in the past we might have said that an apathetic response is grounded in yielding or avoiding conflict, we see it differently now. During the pandemic, many employees built up personal protective barriers to deal with the pain of loss, a fear of the future, and the new reality of what is important in life. These protective barriers combine to create behaviors at work that can result in not being engaged enough to notice conflict. We believe that constructive debate is the beginning of the innovation and change process—and apathy has a real opportunity cost. The COVID-19 pandemic has had a profound impact on the dynamics of conflict in several ways, and I'm not sure anyone knows the full impact yet:

1. *Stress and anxiety.* The uncertainty, fear, and disruptions caused by the pandemic have increased stress and anxiety levels worldwide. Elevated stress levels can heighten emotional reactivity and decrease impulse control. This potentially exacerbates conflicts in various settings including work, home, and our communities.

2. *Social isolation.* The landscape for working from home has been permanently altered. Lockdowns, social distancing measures, and remote work have led to increased social isolation and reduced opportunities for in-person interactions. Lack of social support and increased feelings of loneliness can contribute to heightened emotional distress and interpersonal conflicts.

3. *Economic stress.* The economic fallout of the pandemic, including job losses, financial insecurity, and business closures (or the constant fear of those), has exacerbated socioeconomic disparities and increased financial stress for many individuals and families. Economic strain can fuel conflicts over resources, financial decisions, and household responsibilities.

4. *Health concerns and disruption of social norms.* The threat of COVID-19 transmission and concerns about personal and family health have intensified workplace conflicts over adherence to public health guidelines, vaccination decisions, and health care access. Disagreements about

risk mitigation strategies and differing perceptions of the pandemic's severity can strain relationships and communities.

5. *Political polarization.* The pandemic has further polarized societies with conflicting beliefs, attitudes, and responses to public health measures and government interventions. Divisive rhetoric, misinformation, and conspiracy theories have fueled ideological conflicts and eroded trust in institutions, exacerbating social tensions.

6. *Growth in resilience and cooperation.* Despite the challenges, the pandemic has also highlighted the importance of community resilience and cooperation in navigating crises. Never in most of our lifetimes have we engaged in direct human-to-human contact like this, sharing a common experience across all borders. Many communities have come together to support each other, address collective challenges, and find innovative solutions, fostering solidarity and reducing conflict. As HR, have we tapped into this positive outcome enough?

In recent conflict coaching and mediations conducted in the aftermath of the COVID-19 pandemic, a noticeable trend has emerged: employees are facing an increased difficulty in sharing their narratives and expressing their concerns. This phenomenon appears to correlate with the functioning of the Broca area, a region situated in the frontal lobe of the brain that is renowned for its role in language production and speech comprehension.[2] Conflict, whether arising internally or externally, can trigger a cascade of cognitive processes, potentially impacting language and communication skills—a domain where the Broca area plays a pivotal role. The potential effects of conflict on this brain region include the following:

1. *Increased activation.* During conflict resolution, the brain often activates regions involved in decision-making and cognitive control, including the Broca area. This increased activation may reflect the increased demand for language processing and cognitive resources required to resolve the conflict.

2. *Impaired language production.* High levels of conflict or stress can impair cognitive functions, including language production mediated by the Broca area. This might manifest as difficulty finding words, stuttering, or other speech disruptions.

3. *Cognitive control impacts.* Conflict can interfere with cognitive control processes, including those mediated by the Broca area, leading to difficulties in organizing and articulating thoughts coherently.

4. *Brain connections.* Conflict may alter the connectivity

---

2 Bessel van der Kolk, *The Body Keeps the Score: Brain, Mind, and Body in the Healing of Trauma* (New York: Viking, 2014).

patterns between the Broca area and other brain regions involved in cognitive control and emotional regulation. This altered connectivity could impact language processing and production abilities.

5. *Different starting points.* Different individuals may show varying susceptibility to the effects of conflict on the Broca area depending on factors such as stress resilience, cognitive flexibility, and overall brain health.

The specific effects of conflict may vary depending on the nature and intensity of the conflict, as well as individual differences in cognitive functioning. These responses can be especially embarrassing and frustrating to our employees, who may otherwise be both articulate and logical. Our ability to "slow the room" to let our employees gather their thoughts in conflict conversations is the best gift we can give to our employees—and the strategies in this book all take this problem into account.

AI and Conflict

In the wake of significant societal events like COVID-19, another force looms large on the horizon: artificial intelligence (AI). We believe that AI tools will offer both opportunities and challenges in relation to conflict resolution. AI tools can help track and resolve conflicts, provide insights into root causes, enhance communication that can ultimately establish trust, and even produce creative solutions to conflicts—all in a relatively unbiased manner. Some mediation experts, for example, already believe that technology is the "fourth person in the room" and embrace it as such.

However, there are challenges that current HR professionals will—not might—be navigating. While AI can analyze vast amounts of complex information, it may struggle with the subtle nuances and emotional aspects of conflicts that humans can understand. Will our near-future workforces engage with AI that will respond with only logical thought? And how will we navigate conflicts when our human employees use that very logical information to "prove" their point of view? Despite the benefits, we foresee inevitable workplace conflicts as debates occur regarding biases in algorithms. We foresee these impacts very soon:

1. *Accountability.* The development and deployment of AI in conflict scenarios raises complex ethical and legal questions regarding accountability, transparency, and adherence to international humanitarian law. Concerns about autonomous decisions without human intervention, alone, raise the risk of unintended consequences and potential violations of human rights.

2. *Social tensions.* AI-driven automation is currently transforming labor markets and industries, leading to economic dislocation and social unrest. In regions heavily

reliant on industries vulnerable to AI disruption, such as manufacturing or transportation, economic inequalities and job displacement may fuel social tensions and conflicts over resources and opportunities.

3. *Peacebuilding.* On a positive note, AI technologies hold potential for mitigating conflicts and promoting peacebuilding efforts. AI algorithms can analyze vast amounts of data to identify early warning signs of conflicts, facilitate humanitarian aid distribution, or support mediation and negotiation processes by providing insights into conflict dynamics and potential solutions. Harnessing AI as an idea generator could prove invaluable in fostering peace amid turbulent times efficiently!

When it comes to dealing with AI in the workplace, HR professionals will soon play a vital role in facilitating the integration of AI alongside human workers. Here are some key ways HR professionals can help in managing the interaction between humans and AI:

1. *Grow our HR knowledge set.* If we will ultimately manage both a human and robot workforce with an AI backdrop working faster than we possibly can, we will need to have a deep understanding of human-machine interaction and collaboration methods to ensure a smoother integration of AI into the workplace.

2. *Facilitate training programs.* This is how HR professionals can equip employees with the necessary skills to work alongside AI effectively, such as troubleshooting issues and collaborating with automated systems.

3. *Develop communication plans and policies.* These plans and policies can address the realistic concerns about job displacement due to automation. To prevent unmanageable conflicts, HR will help with clear communication, transparency, and support during transitions.

As we move from dealing with COVID-19 to figuring out AI's impact, one thing is certain: we need to be flexible and creative. Just a year ago, the idea of incorporating discussions on AI applications into our book's introduction or contemplating the influence of robot-assisted conflict resolution would have seemed far-fetched. While many questions remain unanswered, it is clear that HR professionals play a pivotal role in enabling workplaces to navigate uncertainties and maintain effective communication during ongoing transformations. Embracing this challenge is how we all pitch in to create a future that's both peaceful and lasting.

Proactive Conflict Resolution

Imagine a workplace where diverse perspectives aren't just tolerated, but celebrated; where conflicts aren't viewed as roadblocks, but as opportunities for growth and innovation. Picture a scenario where every encounter, whether it's a brainstorming session or a team meeting, becomes a springboard for deeper understanding and collaboration. This isn't just a lofty ideal—it's a necessity in today's rapidly evolving landscape.

Consider a scenario where a team is tasked with developing a new marketing strategy. In this hypothetical situation, individuals from various departments come together, each with their own unique insights and approaches. Initially, excitement fills the room as ideas are tossed around freely. As discussions progress, conflicting viewpoints emerge, leading to tension and frustration among team members. Without effective conflict resolution strategies in place, the once-promising brainstorming session devolves into a stalemate, hindering progress and eroding team morale.

Now, envision a different outcome. In this scenario, the team is equipped with the tools and techniques necessary to navigate conflicts constructively. When differing opinions arise, instead of resorting to arguments or disengagement, team members engage in respectful dialogue, actively listening to one another's perspectives and seeking common ground. Through open communication and a commitment to understanding, the team not only resolves their differences but also emerges stronger and more united than before. As a result, they're able to develop a comprehensive marketing strategy that incorporates a wide range of ideas and perspectives, ultimately leading to greater success for the organization.

This is where you, as HR professionals, play a pivotal role. By fostering a culture that values open dialogue, embraces diversity of thought, and prioritizes restorative conversations, you have the power to transform conflicts into opportunities for growth and collaboration. Whether it's mediating disputes between colleagues, facilitating team-building exercises, or implementing training programs on conflict resolution skills, your proactive approach can help shape a workplace where differences are not only accepted, but celebrated.

In the pages that follow, we'll do a deep dive into the principles and practices of effective conflict resolution, providing you with actionable strategies and real-world examples to empower you in your role. Together, we'll explore how you can cultivate a culture of constructive debate, navigate polarizing discussions with grace and empathy, and ultimately build stronger, more resilient teams. We'll also shed light on the pivotal role of HR, often called upon to stand in the gap during conflicts by facilitating communication, fostering understanding, and mediating resolutions to promote a harmonious workplace environment.

Critical Thinking Questions

1. How can an awareness of the brain's emotional and cognitive process, as well as hormonal influences, help you with your approach to conflict resolution in the workplace?

2. From your own experiences, how has the COVID-19 pandemic affected the landscape of workplace conflicts?

3. Considering the evolving landscape of conflicts due to factors like COVID-19 and advancements in AI technology, how can you as an HR professional remain flexible and creative in your conflict resolution approaches?

Shifting Your Mindset

Sammie glances at the calendar and there it is again: the XYZ budget lead, Jordan, as the first appointment of the day, and Sammie is sure Jordan will complain again about the lack of respect being paid to money boundaries on the team. Sammie is just sick of it because it feels like every idea raised has to go through this "we don't have the money" and "how much will that cost" debate. As Jordan arrives, Sammie gets ready to argue that it is too early in the recent project to talk about money. Sammie is shocked when Jordan says, "You know, Sammie, you are the lead, and I'm not going to raise money issues again unless you ask. I'm sorry if I've disrespected you." Sammie grabs what feels like a great win, and graciously says, "I know you're just doing your job." It feels like a great meeting, except months later during a status update the steering group looks at the top three emerging ideas from the team and says they're floored by the cost. The steering group demands to know why no conversation or preplanning for the currently unrealistic ideas occurred. Sammie leaves that meeting and immediately calls Jordan. Jordan says of course the ideas are unrealistic with the current budget structure, but Sammie didn't ask and that was the agreement between them. This is a classic example of yielding or compromising too soon during the early phases of change efforts—and this, along with other harmful conflict responses, can easily derail an entire project.

Let's embark on a transformative journey by reshaping your perspective on the advantages of conflict within the workplace. As human resources professionals, you wield significant influence as agents of change. Consider this: conflict serves as the catalyst for evolution and progress. Absent opposing viewpoints or spirited debates, we risk succumbing to the perils of groupthink. While harmonious interactions may seem ideal, they often stifle innovation and hinder collaborative decision-making. Our objective is to harness the constructive potential of conflict by channeling our focus toward the task at hand rather than toward interpersonal discord. This endeavor, though seemingly straightforward in theory, proves challenging in practice. This is precisely where your role as an HR professional becomes indispensable—you facilitate constructive dialogue, guide individuals toward productive conflict resolution, and ultimately shape the cultural fabric of organizations through your interventions.

Employees most often come to you for help when they've already tried to work things out or they are conflict-avoidant. They come to HR because they want your intervention. It's often a profoundly vulnerable space for them, and the first step in being trusted to help is for you to become competent. Your competence leads to confidence, and employees in conflict will notice that confidence and begin to relax into problem-solving.

Looking back to when we began in the HR and alternative dispute resolution field as mediators, we started our work with a legalistic mindset. While we entered into the work to engage with conflict at the earliest and lowest level possible within organizations, the truth was that what we meant by that is we wanted to resolve conflict before it led to costly formal actions or to resolve those already formally levied grievances with mediation and coaching instead of investigations. We were only partially on the right path with this mindset. We still agree that a facilitated approach—where the employee has an active part in resolving formal actions—is often better than an investigation that ends with the feeling that someone is winning and someone else is losing. After working with many clients, we realized that frontline leaders and human resources staff could not have intervened earlier in the conflict. What if the conflict in front of us were channeled to a better path, instead of just handled by tamping it down? How many employees had to witness or hear about or be otherwise impacted by the entrenched conflict before someone intervened? What was the opportunity cost?

The cost of conflicts to the organization in terms of innovative debate is a big deal. Change models have traditionally been linear: in other words, getting from here to there. Change was managed as an input-to-output process with little attention paid to team dynamics. The input process had a beginning, when a team was chartered by identifying goals and key stakeholders; the team was staffed and assembled; a project plan was developed with milestones and due dates; and then ideas about how to achieve the goal went through rigorous documentation, facilitation, and narrowing by trained project managers. Through efforts like Total Quality Management and Lean Six Sigma and similar project planning methodologies, we examined how to be efficient and effective. Most of the attention in these efforts was paid to timelines and output goals.

With the rise of the internet and globalization, changes began happening more rapidly and sometimes even chaotically. New approaches to innovation processes recognized the need to be quicker, so project managers and leaders felt the need to focus attention on further processes to help with decision-making and risk management. Not quite sure what to do with these human behaviors and many times conflict-avoidant, the idea was that if employees could just be encouraged to deliver results by paying attention to output processes, team dynamics would be optimized through the feeling of accomplishment. Brainstorming tools could be used to debate ideas to keep everyone focused and that work could be included on a strict timeline, and any other underlying conflict was often ignored or even disciplined. "Time is money" became a common refrain.

But there is a shift happening now, because more and more companies are recognizing that their true competitive edge is contained within the brains of their workforce. Leading human resources is no longer the job of a department but is the responsibility of leaders, project managers, and professional human resources experts. We know about this recognition not because of research (although it exists), but because these project leaders and managers are showing up in the same human behavior coaching technique classes, conferences, and workshops as human resources experts. Suddenly, there is a whole lot of attention paid to team dynamics and how we enter into the change process. You won't get very far into a coaching workshop before the topic of conflict comes up, and this subject is very often raised by project leaders and managers who are seeking HR experts to help.

The first shift, then, is to shift your mindset about change. Traditionally, we are taught to think about conflict in two ways: conflict is interpersonal (we just need to get along), or it is costing money so we should tamp it down fast. As we saw in the chapter's opening anecdote, when we yield or compromise too quickly on important issues like budget, we can end up with a result later in the project implementation that can be derailing. If Sammie and Jordan had spent more time in constructive debate on pros and cons, perhaps Sammie could have seen Jordan's budget concerns as valid points. That "get along" mindset limits opportunities to harness the power of conflict for good. Taking a stand for the benefits of conflict means that you must not only conceptually believe conflict is beneficial, but you also need to be able to articulate a new change model to your workforce. Here is that change model:

CONFLICT SPARKS CHANGE: A DYNAMIC MODEL

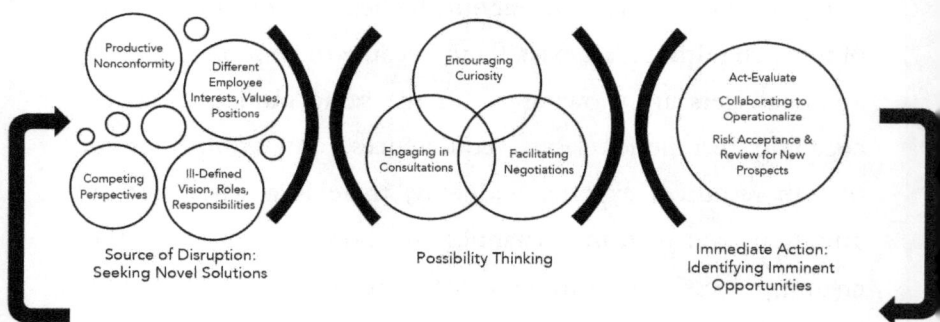

In this model, the first observation is there are differences in ideas, concepts, or opinions, alongside a spirit of curiosity and healthy debate, which forms its foundation. What sets this model apart is its emphasis on devoting equal attention and time to the initial phase of change, where various sources of disruption are recognized as a necessary catalyst for change. Understanding how and why ideas are generated or dismissed is as important as meeting deadlines, which typically receive the most focus in many organizations. Merely striving for diversity in hiring or staffing isn't sufficient; HR experts must advocate for diverse thinking tools to foster robust debate, or else the efforts in hiring will be futile.

Enhancing your expertise as an HR leader necessitates gaining proficiency in the first part of the change model—source disruptions—which involves learning additional conflict resolution strategies outlined in this book. The reason? Teaching employees conflict management skills benefits every stage of the model, as each idea debated in subsequent stages relies on supporting and channeling the inevitable yet beneficial conflicts that arise in the initial phase of change. Your objective as an HR professional is to navigate the workforce through conflict consistently. Let's delve deeper into how conflict manifests within each stage of the model.

HR TIP: Imagery can be very useful in conflict. We keep several sets of 4x6 picture cards and pull them out when clients are unable to articulate how it feels to be in conflict or what a great team atmosphere would be like.

Source Disruptions

The source disruptions stage in conflict tells us something new is unfolding. Conceptually, we have just a few ways to handle conflict: (1) fight it out until someone wins, (2) avoid it, (3) compromise or yield, or (4) activate it to capitalize on conflict's benefits. Fighting it out in the workplace is draining and damaging, and it is often impossible to tell who won. Avoiding conflict leads to a whole host of problems—simmering until explosion, quitting on the clock, opportunity costs, and mediocre thinking. Compromise may be necessary to move forward, but it's yielding to the point that later down the road, you're building upon a situation that began as a lose-lose proposition. The other concern with compromise is that it kicks conflict down the road. After all, when something doesn't turn out well, the other party will say, "We should have gone with my idea in the first place." We rarely let go of an idea that is compromised. It's only the last possibility—activating conflict—that makes a difference in the beginning of change.

When the disruption is simply a strong hold on competing ideas, we can channel this by learning about respecting others' ideas and building upon them, rather than simply restating ours. We have four great and simple ideas for encouraging teams to welcome and respect new ideas.

1. Employees must demonstrate and encourage respect for new ideas. One effective way to do this is by consistently acknowledging the positive aspects of an idea before adding further thoughts or criticisms. For example, immediately after an idea is presented, the leader or coworker could say, "I like [specific aspect] about that idea," before offering additional input. Similarly, when someone builds upon the initial idea, they should also begin by highlighting what they appreciate about it before expanding upon it.

2. Foster a more inclusive and respectful environment for capturing ideas in group settings, especially during times of change. Two examples—

- *Avoiding the "parking lot" metaphor.* Using phrases like "let's put that idea in the parking lot" can inadvertently signal that certain ideas are being set aside or dismissed. Instead, employing imagery like the refrigerator encourages a more positive and inclusive approach. By visualizing ideas as items stored in a refrigerator, it conveys the message that these ideas are valued and preserved for future consideration, rather than being forgotten or discarded. Emphasizing the team's responsibility to pull ideas out before they go stale reinforces a collaborative mindset where everyone plays a role in nurturing and developing ideas.

- *Respectful summarization of ideas.* When summarizing ideas, it's important to ensure that the essence of each idea is accurately captured. Simply asking if the idea has been represented in a way that aligns with the originator's intention demonstrates respect for their contribution. This approach acknowledges the diverse perspectives within the group and affirms each individual's unique contribution to the discussion.

3. Translate commitment to teamwork into concrete actions that support daily collaborative efforts. For instance, during the initial stages of team formation, it's common

for members to seek the leader's attention. While it's natural for employees to desire recognition, excessive individual attention can be detrimental. As a leader, valuing teamwork means acknowledging individual contributions while immediately redirecting focus to the team. When an employee shares their work, it's essential to inquire about their collaborators and invite them all to a meeting to discuss progress and celebrate achievements together. Similarly, when recognizing employee contributions, it helps to prioritize team achievements over individual ones to avoid fostering competitiveness and potential conflicts among team members.

4. Navigate role ambiguity and overlapping tasks. When the source disruptions are not about competing ideas but are behaviorally focused, things get trickier. There may be confusion about roles and responsibilities, as this is a common source of workplace conflict. Despite efforts to assemble a skilled team, modern work environments, especially those reliant on knowledge, involve fluid roles and tasks that often overlap. While avoiding duplicated efforts is important for cost efficiency, the real concern lies in the conflicts arising from role ambiguity. No one wants to invest effort only to find it duplicated by a team member. However, acknowledging that such conflicts are inevitable helps mitigate them through effective communication. It falls on leaders to regularly inquire about task

ownership and foster a culture of collaboration where team members share updates and successes, facilitating the detection and resolution of duplicated efforts.

In the next potential source in the disruption stage, conflicts can arise from differences in how employees value and manage their work. These discrepancies in interests, values, and approaches to teamwork often become apparent in teams with diverse compositions. Such differences are commonly referred to as varying work ethics, although this terminology can be misleading. Some employees prioritize work as a central aspect of their lives, while others may not place as much emphasis on it. There are employees who are politically savvy or strive for recognition to advance in the organizational hierarchy, while others may view such behaviors as sycophantic or narcissistic. These differing perspectives can lead to tensions within the team. Conflicts may also arise from employees coming from diverse cultural backgrounds or different eras where values such as loyalty, hard work, and commitment are emphasized differently. These disparities can lead to clashes over the interpretation and importance of these values in the workplace.

HR TIP: During onboarding, be intentional about discussing behavior norms that align with the organization's mission and value statements. If perseverance is a key value, for example, tie that to how you deal with conflict.

It's astonishing to witness how organizations, in their sincere efforts to foster team cohesion and personal development, inadvertently sow seeds of divisiveness that can lead to conflict. Have you ever participated in a workshop or course that broadly categorizes generations, such as millennials and baby boomers, with sweeping generalizations? Or perhaps you've taken an assessment that assigns you a label, supposedly for better understanding behavior within a team, only to find that it differs significantly from someone else's label and explains away your problem communicating with that person. What's concerning is that this penchant for labeling individuals creates a dangerous dichotomy of "us versus them" thinking. When we start categorizing others and attributing motives to their actions based on these labels, we veer away from discussing the task at hand, inviting interpersonal conflicts to take center stage. Even when these labels could offer valuable insights into team dynamics, facilitators often fail to provide guidance on how to navigate conflicts that arise from these differences. Instead, employees often adopt a passive stance, attributing conflicts to immutable characteristics, saying, "This is just the way they are," instead of actively engaging in resolving conflicts that stem from differences.

While the intention behind these activities may be to enhance team cohesion and personal development, the unintended consequence is often the reinforcement of divisive thinking patterns that hinder collaboration and breed conflict. Organizations need to recognize and address these pitfalls to foster a more inclusive and harmonious work environment. Here are two tips:

1. Be extremely cautious about who you select to facilitate team-building activities. As an HR professional, you hold the responsibility of being the gatekeeper in this regard. It's up to you to decide whether facilitated assessments, coaching, and team-building exercises will be beneficial for a team in conflict or whether you need to engage in rigorous debate of new ideas. You also have the discretion to determine if gaining a deeper understanding of each other's personality types is necessary. It's essential to conduct thorough research and not assume that your employees are well-versed in the social sciences and understand how to use these labels effectively. We've observed instances where employees—and even leaders—have used their personality type labels to justify their behavior, saying things like, "I'm a [insert label], so you need to understand this about me. This label explains why I act the way I do."

2. Bring individuals in conflict into a mediation (facilitated dialogue) quickly. This facilitated dialogue serves a vital purpose, as evidenced by the existence of comprehensive strategies for conducting such conversations. The phrase "misery loves company" holds true in this context. It reflects the observation that conflicts tend to escalate rapidly within teams as individuals attempt to rally support for their viewpoints. While some may label this behavior as gossip, it's essential to recognize that gossip often serves as a communication channel rooted in underlying conflicts.

Yet another disruption has to do with different innovation styles. This pertains to how individuals within a team approach and engage with new ideas. Instead of categorizing employees, it's important to recognize that some people are more inclined to be agreeable to others' ideas while others tend to challenge them. A successful team benefits from a balance of both types, as each brings unique perspectives and contributes to the innovation process. In terms of managing conflict, individuals who prefer to test ideas before accepting them often exhibit a strong inclination toward nonconformity. This means that they tend to subject every idea to rigorous scrutiny and analysis, often pointing out potential flaws or weaknesses before deeming it acceptable. While this approach is not inherently obstructive, it may be perceived as such, leading to misunderstandings or negative judgments.

To address this, the term "productive nonconformists" is introduced in the change model, emphasizing the importance of having at least one such individual on any team focused on innovative thinking. It's a better term than "devil's advocates," which can sound off-putting or combative; the more helpful label of "productive nonconformists" reflects a future-oriented stance that more fully captures the positive intent behind these types of employee actions. Rather than relying solely on processes like brainstorming to prevent groupthink, try deliberately considering and discussing innovation styles during the team formation stage. Without someone who challenges ideas in the early disruption stage, there's a risk of groupthink stifling creativity and critical thinking.

It's also essential to manage the potential frustration and conflicts that arise from these nonconforming innovation types. One strategy is to teach them to acknowledge and respect others' ideas before offering counterpoints, which can help prevent them from being perceived as obstinate. Fostering open and continuous discussions within the team about the value of counterpoints encourages a culture of constructive criticism and collaboration. When counterpoints are raised they should be publicly acknowledged and welcomed, reinforcing their importance in the innovation process.

There are so many more opportunities for disruptions, but whatever the source, your mindset about how important they are to creating a learning, idea-focused organization is essential. Conflict sparks change because it is the part of the model where two perspectives don't align yet, and something new is trying to emerge. Constructive controversy leads to creativity, and channeling conflict to achieve it is an HR leader's big job for advocating for this type of creative environment.

Possibility Thinking

Once you've set up a culture that supports conflict and idea sharing seems like it is going pretty well, you might think your work with channeling conflict is done. But you'll realize that conflict shows up again. As employees settle in on exploring one or more ideas as "leading thoughts" for the moment, it is natural that they begin to align with one or the other ideas about the way forward. Successful facilitation helps to harness the positive benefits of conflict in this section of the model when we—

1. *Establish a culture of conflict and idea sharing.* Initially, the focus is on creating an organizational culture that encourages open communication, idea sharing, and constructive conflict resolution. This lays the groundwork for effective collaboration and innovation within the team or organization.

2. *Notice continued conflict in the idea exploration phase.* Even after successfully fostering a culture of open communication, conflicts can resurface during the phase of exploring various ideas. This occurs as team members naturally gravitate toward different concepts or solutions, leading to diverging viewpoints and potential tensions.

3. *Actively facilitate conflict resolution.* Effective facilitation becomes important during this phase to manage conflicts and maintain focus on the task at hand. Various tools such as force field analysis, brainstorming, mind mapping, affinity diagrams, and Ishikawa diagrams are employed to guide discussions and align team members' perspectives.

4. *Teach process.* The use of multiple tools highlights the meticulous attention paid to the process of idea exploration and conflict resolution. Each tool serves a specific purpose in helping team members express their thoughts

and opinions while ensuring that the discussion remains productive and focused.

5. *Carry over and expand upon team behavior norms.* It's emphasized that the positive team behavior norms established in the earlier stages must be maintained throughout the process. This includes respecting diverse ideas and perspectives, regardless of whether they align with one's own.

6. *Purposefully integrate new team members.* When new members join the team, it's essential to integrate them into the existing team dynamics and ensure they understand and adhere to the established norms of respectful communication and collaboration.

Through the use of force field analysis, brainstorming, mind mapping, affinity diagrams, Ishikawa diagrams, and other similar tools, team members stay focused on the work but also feel like their thoughts are included. Can you see how much (good) attention has been paid to process with all these tools? The model reminds you that we must carry over team behavior norms of respecting ideas now in place from the work done in the first stage. One caution here is that when new team members are introduced, attention to teaming behaviors with the new team members and existing team members is necessary. How will you, as the HR expert, facilitate this and help the team talk about their vision for teamwork?

During this phase, as the team delves into specific ideas, collaboration with various departments becomes essential. Consultations with resource departments, technology experts, and others may be required—potentially introducing further conflict, especially if key stakeholders disagree. It's important to prepare team members for these encounters by helping them anticipate responses from stakeholders, both positive and negative.

We advocate for integrating negotiation skills into foundational employee training. Engaging in endless debates can drain team energy and escalate tensions when progress stalls. While various methodologies exist, it's essential to tailor the training to individual employees rather than adopting a one-size-fits-all approach. Establishing a shared language and process and fostering active listening skills empowers each team member to anticipate and navigate the negotiation process effectively. Employees can support each other, particularly when someone lacks polished negotiation skills. Implementing this integrated training initiative, spearheaded by the HR department, can address power imbalances within the team. While we often associate power imbalances with positional authority, they can manifest in various ways. Strong personalities or individuals with a results-driven focus may dominate discussions, overshadowing quieter team members or those averse to conflict. Equipping all employees with negotiation skills fosters a more balanced dynamic, mitigating unproductive conflicts and yielding substantial benefits for the organization.

In your capacity as the HR expert, your pivotal role extends beyond traditional administrative tasks. You are entrusted with the responsibility of fostering a cohesive and harmonious work environment by orchestrating discussions that center around teamwork and aligning the team's vision. Your multifaceted duties encompass a spectrum of activities aimed at enhancing collaboration, communication, and conflict resolution within the team. As a facilitator, you utilize your specialized knowledge on human behaviors when you orchestrate various team-building exercises and workshops designed to fortify bonds among team members, cultivate effective communication channels, and equip individuals with conflict resolution skills. Through these interactive sessions, you strive to nurture a culture of mutual respect, understanding, and synergy.

Your role transcends mere facilitation; you serve as a pillar of support and guidance for both seasoned veterans and newcomers within the team. Whether it's providing mentorship to new recruits or offering advice to existing members who are navigating challenges, you play an integral part in ensuring every team member feels empowered and valued. And as the organizational landscape evolves, so too does the role of HR. In today's dynamic environment, HR professionals are increasingly called upon to actively engage in change management processes. This evolution necessitates a proactive approach wherein HR professionals not only facilitate discussions, but also actively participate in steering organizational transformations.

The strategies delineated in this book serve as invaluable tools to aid you in your journey—and essential to their efficacy is a recognition of the evolving nature of HR's role. Embracing this evolution empowers you to not only facilitate discussions but also spearhead transformative initiatives, thereby driving organizational growth and success.

Implementation

This is the part of the model that has undoubtedly received the most attention in other change models. Here we need to decide the way forward by weighing the risks against the benefits. This is also where negativity or positivity bias occurs, and bias does cause conflict between employees. Sometimes team members are hesitant to implement for fear of failure. This is also where the pressure to produce gets significant. Emotions rule as employees become weary from the work, overly excited, relieved, and sometimes apprehensive that the project will stick. These conflicting emotions cause conflict among team members, and when you add on the external pressures from key stakeholders (it seems like everyone has an opinion on what to do), it can be frustrating and exhausting. Frustration and exhaustion lead to acting out, even among great team members.

This is why we believe, in this final stage, we need to take the word "decision" completely out of the picture because the word implies a permanent, unchanging state. What happens is that we act and evaluate. We collaborate and operationalize. The minute we do so, no matter how well we've done in the rest of the model, we will soon see the need to reevaluate and change something else. What else, after we implement, will we learn? What shows up in this new way of doing or thinking about something? Which outcomes will mean some ideas are not implemented? This is where a learning and curious team, led by a leader championing the idea of continuous rethinking and idea generation, will level up once again. Since the final stage of change is fraught with emotions, HR has the responsibility to know this and seek out facilitation and training that will help the team move forward.

In this stage, it is helpful to learn critical thinking processes that help reduce choice. We each have our way of approaching choices, and that can cause us to have individual blinders. Just as employees have individual levels of comfort in taking risks, employees also apply critical thinking differently. We encourage you to take the word "bias" and change it to "critical thinking" by implementing processes that require an evaluation process before and after an output is operationalized. If you've taken the step to add nonconformists to your teams, how are you supporting them as they voice differing opinions? When employees are starting to see light at the end of the tunnel, are you asking, "What are other possible opinions?" Sometimes, these other opinions lead you to implement temporarily and enter right back into the change model. Other times, it is the competing opinions that help you evaluate ideas by building in "what if" questions. Perhaps you've not imagined your HR role in this implementing debate stage, but conflict is there and you should be there too, with expertise and support.

As we transition from this broad strategic perspective to more targeted approaches, it's essential to recognize the pivotal role of your expertise in HR conflict resolution in driving successful organizational change. If you've previously viewed your role solely through the lens of administrative leadership rather than as an active participant in fostering innovation, it's time to reassess. HR professionals serve as custodians of organizational culture, with conflict resolution serving as the litmus test for the manifestation of desired behaviors. Embracing this mindset shift forms the bedrock upon which all subsequent strategies are built. Every conflict, no matter how seemingly insignificant, is a vital component of the change journey. By honing your conflict resolution skills and fostering professional growth, you have the power to effect profound and enduring change in collaboration with your workforce. Embrace this opportunity to harness the transformative potential of conflict and pave the way for a more resilient and adaptive organizational culture.

Critical Thinking Questions

1. When contemplating conflict, which emotions and descriptors immediately come to mind?

2. Upon further reflection, what constructive and uplifting words can you incorporate into your perception of conflict?

3. As an HR professional specializing in conflict intervention, what legacy do you aspire to leave behind (how do you want to be remembered)?

4. What are a few profound quotes about conflict that resonate with you most deeply, serving as enduring pillars of guidance and reflection in your professional journey?

HERE: Steps for a Conflict-Positive Initial Intake Conversation

By the time Lee visits HR to request a mediation, he's frustrated and mad. Despite many feedback meetings with his boss, Amanda, Lee worries that he isn't getting the necessary feedback for career progression. Amanda does not give him clear direction about developmental goals and does not assign Lee tough and important tasks. Lee is giving this problem just one more chance with the mediator's help before he quits the company. In Lee's view, Amanda favors a few employees on the team, and for some reason, Lee is not one of them. Amanda's view is the exact opposite. Equally frustrated, she tells HR that she feels like all she does is talk to Lee, and Lee just doesn't listen. Her view is that Lee doesn't work well on a team and is opinionated, and she regularly tells him that other employees do not enjoy working with him when he is the project leader. Amanda and Lee both agree on one thing: they've had many meetings, and the sessions always end with the same poor result. Amanda believes she gives feedback directly and succinctly, but from her perspective, Lee never learns a thing. Honestly, she's at the point of hoping he does quit, because the entire team's reputation is affected. Lee believes Amanda is a weak leader who can't articulate specific guidance on his tasks, performance, or development.

Of the myriad training initiatives aimed at enhancing workplace communication, encounters marked by frustrating dialogues and unresolved conflicts persist as common workplace challenges. Over more than two decades as practitioners in alternative dispute conflict resolution, we've had the privilege of facilitating the restoration of thousands of workplace relationships, and we've gleaned invaluable insights into uncovering the underlying issues fueling conflicts. Our journey prompted the development of the HERE Conflict Dialogue Model.

This model is not merely theoretical; it's born from real-world conflict resolution and grounded in the understanding that swift, emotionally driven attempts to resolve conflicts often neglect the deeper interests and needs at play. In today's fast-paced work environments, where information flows incessantly and emotions run high, conflicts can swiftly escalate if left unaddressed. Compounding this, employees often exhibit a propensity to avoid confrontation, hindering the establishment of the vital relationship connections necessary for sustainable conflict resolution. Navigating these complexities demands a nuanced understanding and a strategic approach.

It's important to underscore the business imperative behind effective conflict resolution. Every evening, as employees wrap up their day and depart, they carry with them the collective knowledge and capacity essential for driving organizational success. HR professionals understand all too well the necessity of addressing conflicts swiftly and at the lowest possible level. The immediate financial toll of resolving disputes is evident: the precious company time spent in urgent conflict management translates directly into monetary loss. But this is merely the tip of the iceberg. When we delve deeper we uncover numerous additional costs—opportunity costs, increased sick leave, the departure of valuable talent, and the insidious erosion of morale, to name a few. Our conversations with numerous HR directors, along with insights from leadership climate and development surveys, consistently highlight the urgent need for conflict resolution skills development across the organizational spectrum. This is not merely a theoretical concern; it's a palpable reality felt by business leaders and employees alike. Enter our conflict dialogue model—a structured framework designed to facilitate purposeful conversations from the moment of intake. With its guiding questions and emphasis on fostering openness, curiosity, and presence, the HERE approach—Honor the relationship, Explore the story, Reflect, and Enable and Empower—lays the groundwork for efficient yet impactful conflict resolution. While these steps may initially appear time-consuming, our experience has shown them to be surprisingly efficient in navigating and resolving conflicts effectively.

The HERE model represents a paradigm shift in how we perceive and approach conflict scenarios, transcending the realm of purely emotional reactions to cultivate an exploratory mindset. Progress becomes elusive until the emotional turbulence subsides, yet gauging the extent of an employee's emotional state demands our full presence. Many HR professionals possess a theoretical understanding of human biology, but may not routinely navigate its intricacies. Conflict invariably triggers the brain's threat mechanisms. When the amygdala perceives a threat, it swiftly signals the hypothalamus to initiate the fight-or-flight response, while concurrently directing the sensory cortex to deliberate on subsequent actions—a somewhat slower process.[3] The HERE model harnesses this second reaction. By affording employees the space to express themselves without fear of judgment, we cultivate a sense of perceived organizational support—a delicate balance between business imperatives and the human resources driving them. When faced with a convoluted and emotionally charged narrative, it's important to empathize with the employee's experience. By investing time in attentive listening and presence, we not only demonstrate respect but also pave the way for clearer, more actionable insights. By the time conflicts reach the HR desk, employees have likely grappled with them for an extended period, often in heightened emotional states. While overt physiological reactions such as dilated pupils or trembling may signal the

----

3   Bessel van der Kolk, *The Body Keeps the Score: Brain, Mind, and Body in the Healing of Trauma* (New York: Viking, 2014).

activation of the sympathetic nervous system, subtler manifestations like restlessness or disrupted sleep patterns can be equally telling. Left unaddressed, these physiological responses impede clarity of thought and can even jeopardize employee well-being. Fostering an environment conducive to respectful and productive conflict resolution begins with creating optimal conditions for dialogue—an endeavor in which the HERE model serves as a guiding beacon.

Confidentiality

Before delving into the HERE model, it's essential to address a common issue encountered in HR settings: the challenge of maintaining confidentiality when employees request privacy during intake conversations. Frequently, employees may approach HR with a plea for confidentiality, using phrases like, "Can I tell you something in confidence?" Agreeing to such requests can place HR professionals in a precarious position, potentially leading to inaction or breaching agreements made at the outset.

Instead of immediately promising confidentiality, it is advisable to adopt an honest approach. For instance, HR professionals can respond by affirming the employee's initiative in seeking assistance and

> *HR TIP:* Be transparent. Say something like "As a member of the HR team, I'm part of the management structure. My role today is to listen and help us find a way forward."

expressing a commitment to discussing the subsequent steps once the employee has shared their perspective on the matter. As an example, you can simply say, "Thank you for coming to me with this. I appreciate your trust in me by seeking assistance. Before we delve into the details, I want to emphasize that I'm here to support you. What I can promise is an open and honest conversation. Let's start by hearing your perspective on the matter. Once we have a clear understanding, we can discuss the next steps together. Once we've got that down, we can figure out what to do next, together. And just as a heads up, we might need to loop in others to get the best solution."

This approach emphasizes collaboration and acknowledges the possibility of involving additional stakeholders in addressing the issue. The HERE model offers a framework for initiating constructive dialogue, emphasizing key principles such as being profoundly curious to understand, acting in a manner aligned with one's desired legacy, prioritizing seeking perspective over conducting investigations, and envisioning possibilities beyond the immediate narrative, even when the employee's perspective is constrained.

By adopting this approach, several benefits can be realized. First, it introduces the concept of multiple perspectives, laying the groundwork for collaborative problem-solving. Second, it fosters a sense of shared responsibility in charting the way forward. Third, it establishes transparency regarding the potential need to involve others, even if the employee initially prefers to avoid formal complaints.

Questioning Techniques

Various types of questions can be used depending on the stage of the HERE model you are in and the specific needs of the employee involved. Common types of questions and how they can be utilized in conflict coaching include the following:

1. *Open-ended questions.* These encourage the parties to elaborate on their thoughts and feelings. They are valuable for gaining insight into the underlying issues causing conflicts. Do not become overly focused on being open-ended. If you ask a closed (yes/no) question and receive a yes/no answer, simply ask them to tell you more about that from your perspective with questions like—

    • Can you tell me a little more about what happened?

    • How do you feel about the situation?

    • What are your concerns?

2. *Clarifying questions.* These are used to further your understanding of the issues being discussed. They help in avoiding misunderstandings and confusion. For example—

    • When you say [restate it briefly], can you provide me a bit more detail?

    • Can you give me an example?

    • I want to make sure I understand a bit more. From your point of view, are you saying . . . ?

3. *Reflective questions.* These are designed to encourage self-reflection and insight into one's own thoughts and behaviors. They can promote perceived empathy as well. Examples include—

    •   How do you think [what happened] impacted the other person?

    •   How do you think each option aligns with your values and goals?

4. *Evaluative questions.* These are designed to empower employees to take responsibility for their actions and find their own solutions to the conflict. They should be used sparingly so that the intake does not appear to be an investigation. Employees are receptive to these types of questions at their own pace, and it's generally later in the conversation:

    •   What are a few next steps from your perspective?

    •   What support do you need to move forward?

    •   What is your view of the business impact of this conflict?

The best types of questions for conflict coaching will depend on factors such as the nature of the conflict, the personalities involved, and the stage of conflict resolution. A skilled conflict coach will adapt their questioning techniques to suit the specific needs of the individuals they are working with.

The Framework

HERE are the steps you need to take to have a transformational conflict-positive dialogue session and help others to do the same:

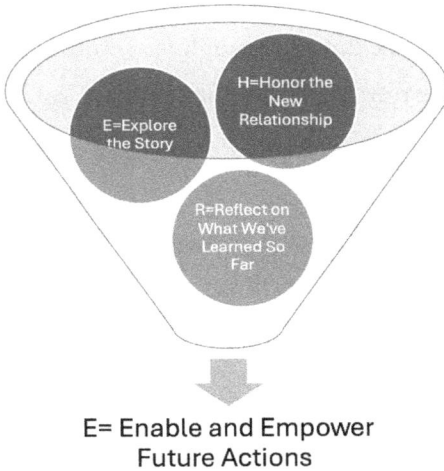

E= Enable and Empower
Future Actions

H—HONOR THE NEW RELATIONSHIP

Taking a few moments before the conflict conversation to choose how you want to be in a relationship with the other person is not only helpful; it is vital. In most conflicts there is a relationship there that you must first acknowledge, even if it's a temporary one. The critical first step toward shifting the relationship to a better space is a bit of self-reflection on how you want to be perceived during, and remembered after, the conversation. Kind? Direct? Honest? One thing that is almost certain: if you approach the conversation from a defensive, critical, or negative posture, you are likely to elicit a similar response.

Honor the relationship by considering your honest response to the following questions:

- What can I do to suspend judgment until I learn more from the other? Am I ready to be reasonably calm, or do I need to talk things through with someone else first so that I don't make the problem worse?

- What can I individually do to create a safe environment, to cooperate and create with the other person, and what will I say upfront to the other person to help them know I am sincere?

- What do I believe we want (current perspective)? What do I imagine the other person wants?

- Am I truly committed to trying to work on both the problem and the relationship?

HR TIP: Sometimes it's hard for an employee to know where to begin. Try starting HERE conversations like this: "Why don't you begin with telling me what was happening right before you decided to call HR?"

When you are ready, someone has to reach out first! Take the time to work on these questions together, knowing that if you are the initiator, the other person may need time to feel safe enough to share:

- Do we agree to work hard to suspend judgment until we learn more from each other?

- What can we do to create a safe environment to cooperate and create with each other?

- What has happened, and what do we believe we want and need (current perspective on the issue)?

- Are we truly committed to trying to work on the problem and relationship?

E—EXPLORE THE STORY

Exploring begins with acknowledging differences that exist without focusing on fault or possible results yet. In this step, the focus is on the opportunity to learn and create by discussing similarities and differences of positions. Ideally, each person will consider the other person's perspectives and adapt their position as they hear new information. Perspective taking is much like trying on a new coat when someone says it would look good on you—you don't have to buy the coat, you just need to take it long enough to try it on. Even if you don't buy that particular coat, you may have a broader perspective about other coats in the future that you might not have considered before. In that way, perspective seeking grows the skill to seek perspective. Allow space for emotions in this phase, and name those that are present.

Key questions to explore:

- What do we know for sure because we have evidence (facts)?

- What do we believe to be true, but we can't be totally sure?

- What is working well?

- What are the challenges? What angers us the most?

R—REFLECT

Reflecting is the step that allows you to both seek clarity and challenge assumptions. This key step is the tough part if you've done the previous steps well because this is when you finally have enough information, and perhaps courage, to focus on resolving the issue through joint dialogue.

Take time here to consider the following:

- What do we know now that we did not know before we took the time to communicate—what is our deeper awareness?

- What do we agree needs to be addressed as a result of what we know to lead to a resolution?

- What do we want or need to change in the relationship so that we can move forward (be made whole)?

E—ENABLE AND EMPOWER

This is the results stage where you draft action steps that you will commit to, and you discuss how you will hold each other accountable. It is essential to co-generate ideas and create solutions with a future focus. When objections or pessimistic outlooks surface, they are discussed and conquered together.

Key questions in this phase include:

- What's possible now?
- What do we intend to do next?
- When will we meet again?
- How can we help each other with the next steps?
- How do we both (all) feel now?
- How do we end this conversation?

As you embark on these conversations regarding conflict scenarios, your foremost objective is to foster a sense of presence and dialogue. Rather than assuming the role of an interrogator, approach the situation as a supportive HR representative committed to facilitating resolution. When employees seek out HR they may arrive feeling disheartened, yet they have taken a proactive step toward resolution by reaching out. We view a HERE session as one of the most intimate professional encounters within the workplace: a structured dialogue that transcends mere verbal exchange. The prevalence of conflict similar to those experienced by Lee and Amanda in our opening scenario underscores the tangible costs incurred—wasted time, squandered opportunities, and deteriorating morale. The HERE approach holds the potential to reframe challenging conversations as opportunities for growth, healing, and sustainable solutions.

Critical Thinking Questions

1. Which parts of the HERE model resonate with you immediately, and why?

2. Are there elements of the model with which you disagree, and how would you approach those stages differently?

3. What are some questions that you could incorporate into each stage of the model, drawing from your own experience and expertise?

4. Do you genuinely believe in your ability to cultivate a space of nonjudgmental presence during conflict conversations? If so, how might this benefit you as an HR consultant? If not, what steps can you take to enhance your listening skills and resist the urge to immediately jump into problem-solving mode?

SORTED: A Framework for Capturing Conflict Narratives

By the time Ben visits Thomas—a seasoned dispute resolution human resources professional—to request mediation, he is frustrated and confused. Sandy, Ben's valued employee, approached him regarding a conflict she was having with a coworker that she described as bullying. Thomas, as good conflict professionals do, asks Ben a few high-level questions to get started and is prepared to listen before recommending anything. Right away, a familiar picture emerges when Ben pulls out his legal pad with plenty of notes. The flipping back and forth between pages of statements makes Thomas wonder what Ben must look like to his employee Sandy, because all these notes indicate he was conducting an inquiry instead of listening. Though not lacking in details from Ben, Thomas lacks contextual understanding about what occurred—and as he's trying to sort the situation out, he's feeling information overload.

Despite the plethora of well-intentioned training programs and interventions geared toward assisting leaders, a critical component of conflict resolution often remains overlooked: how to effectively take notes during conflict discussions without detracting from active listening and presence. While HR training commonly emphasizes the importance of taking good notes, the definition of what constitutes helpful notes frequently eludes practitioners. Drawing from our extensive experience in conducting conflict resolution interventions, we recognized a significant gap in existing practices and devised the SORTED model, a structured framework designed to streamline the intake process and distill complex conflict narratives into manageable components.

At its core, the SORTED model not only serves as a tool for simplifying complex conflict conversations but also emphasizes the importance of de-complexifying the discourse itself. By breaking down intricate conflicts into manageable components, this model enables clearer understanding and more effective resolution strategies. Building upon the foundation of the HERE model, which emphasizes openness and curiosity, the SORTED framework adds another layer of practicality by advocating for the maintenance of detailed notes.

The act of de-complexifying conversations involves several key steps:

1. *Breaking things down.* Dividing the conversation into distinct segments or themes helps in focusing on individual aspects of the conflict, making it easier to analyze and address them effectively.

2. *Structuring information.* Organizing the information gathered from the conversation in a systematic manner involves categorizing points based on relevance, urgency, or stakeholders involved. Organized information is easier to process, and can be referenced efficiently during later stages of conflict resolution.

3. *Reflecting.* HR professionals should reflect on the information gathered and the dynamics observed during the conversation. This reflection fosters deeper insights into the underlying issues and aids in devising appropriate strategies for resolution.

4. *Documenting.* Comprehensive documentation of key points, agreements, and decisions ensures clarity and transparency, serving as a reference point for all parties involved in the conflict resolution process.

5. *Empowering.* By providing a structured framework like SORTED, organizations enable their HR teams to approach conflicts with clarity and competence, ultimately leading to more successful outcomes.

In the realm of HR, where the management of conflicts is critical, having a structured approach like SORTED proves invaluable. It allows HR professionals to distill the essence of complex discussions into concise yet comprehensive records. These records serve as a roadmap for subsequent stages of collaborative problem-solving, ensuring that critical information is not lost or overlooked.

The approach to note-taking outlined within the SORTED framework is characterized by transparency and alignment with legal standards. By clearly indicating that notes are summaries from the employee's perspective and adhering to established organizational practices, HR practitioners can foster a sense of trust and demonstrate genuine attentiveness to employees' concerns. A methodical approach to note-taking encompasses announcing intentions, seeking legal guidance, and clearly documenting the employee's viewpoint.

The Pitfall of Perceived Agreement

Both conflict coaches and mediators often face a common challenge: the risk of assuming agreement when there might not be any. This issue arises from the subtleties of human communication, where something as simple as nodding can be mistakenly interpreted as agreement. Beneath this apparent consensus lies a deeper truth: our emotions heavily influence our perceptions, and significantly affect how we interpret nonverbal cues during conflict resolution. The instinctive reaction to nodding heads can make us feel validated and as if there's agreement, even when genuine consensus is lacking. This dynamic underscores the complex interaction between our rational and emotional faculties in handling conflicts.

To avoid falling into the trap of assuming agreement, conflict coaches and mediators can employ strategic methods. Encouraging open dialogue, clarifying intentions, and actively seeking verbal confirmation are effective ways to ensure real understanding and alignment among all parties involved. By promoting transparent communication, practitioners can reduce the risks of misinterpreting signals. For instance, instead of nodding, it's better to use simple acknowledgments like "I'm tracking" or briefly repeating what was said to demonstrate active listening, such as "so, you felt embarrassed" when the client seeks acknowledgment. Some people might find it helpful to physically restrain themselves from nodding their head by subtly holding their chin during the more emotional conversations.

The Framework

With these principles in mind, we invite you to delve deeper into the intricacies of the SORTED framework, exploring its components and potential applications in navigating complex conflict.

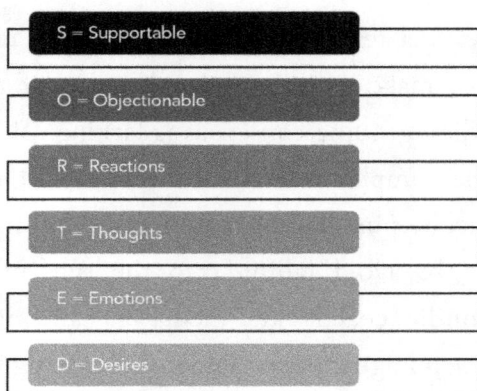

SORTED FRAMEWORK

This framework is best used with the understanding that when dealing with conflicts in the workplace, it's important not to force the conversation into the compartments step by step. Instead, we encourage a flexible and dynamic approach that allows for open dialogue and spontaneity with you taking quick notes within each section as the dialogue flows. The framework requires the need to master this note-taking approach before engaging with employees, as it helps integrate conflict resolution seamlessly into the intake process. By making this flexible framework the primary approach, it promises more efficient conflict resolution through greater clarity after the meeting but still fosters a dynamic dialogue with employees.

S—SUPPORTABLE

In diving into the initial section of our model, we embark upon an exploration of what may initially appear as facts. Here, we meticulously examine the evidence presented, seeking concrete proof such as emails, witness testimonies, documented records, or social media interactions. We pay close attention to whether the information has been explicitly stated by the employee as evidence substantiating their claims.

It is important to approach this section with a discerning mindset. While certain pieces of information may seem like solid information at first glance, it's important to distinguish between what is merely supportable and what can be definitively deemed as fact. The distinction lies in the recognition that the presence of written documentation or verbal assertions does not automatically confer factual status. Instead, it signifies that there is a basis for further investigation and consideration.

This differentiation is important, particularly in conflict resolution scenarios where perceptions may vary and emotions run high. While an employee may interpret certain pieces of evidence as irrefutable proof, our role as HR professionals necessitates a more nuanced understanding. By acknowledging the distinction between supportable information and established facts, we maintain a level of objectivity and rigor in our analysis.

The inclusion of this section in our model serves as a reminder of the need for thorough documentation and consideration of all available evidence. Even if something is not definitively confirmed as fact, its presence in this section signifies its relevance and potential significance in the broader context of the conflict. By upholding a rigorous standard of evaluation and documentation, we ensure that our approach to conflict resolution remains grounded in integrity and fairness, ultimately fostering a more equitable and effective resolution process. Our language as we collect information in this section should reflect that this is from the employee's perspective without being accusatory: "So, from your point of view, the email said that . . . "

The inclusion of the supportable section within the model serves as a valuable checkpoint for later stages of the conflict resolution process. By documenting these sources of information, we create a record of the evidence available, which can inform further investigation and analysis. While it may not represent conclusive proof, the presence of supportable information prompts us to consider its relevance and potential implications for the resolution process. Your questions are guided by—

- Is there direct evidence—emails, witnesses, documentation, social media?
- Has the information been stated by the employee as proof?

As we populate this section of the model, we do so with a keen awareness of the nuanced nature of evidence and the potential for misinterpretation. By exercising caution and diligence in our assessment of supportable information, we uphold the integrity of our conflict resolution efforts and ensure that our conclusions are grounded in thorough analysis and objective evaluation.

O—OBJECTIONABLE

This is perhaps the most interesting part of the model for most HR professionals. In this section we focus on documenting the trigger or cause of the conflict as perceived by the employee. This entails capturing essential details such as what events or circumstances served as triggers and what specifically prompted the individual to seek assistance from leadership or HR. Despite the potential for emotional outbursts and the complexity of the narrative, it is important to succinctly record this information in the notes.

By diligently documenting the trigger from the employee's perspective, we demonstrate our commitment to respecting their voice and experiences. Actively listening and accurately summarizing their concerns not only validates their perspective on the experience, but it also provides an opportunity for clarity and reflection. In many cases, our summary may be the first time the individual has had the chance to articulate and understand the specifics of what has troubled them.

While emotions may run high, this section serves to address the more logical aspect of the conflict by identifying the root cause or objection at the heart of the issue. Our ability to capture this information concisely and effectively contributes to a more comprehensive understanding of the conflict dynamics and lays the foundation for subsequent interventions and resolution strategies.

Our role as HR professionals is to navigate through the emotional turmoil and distill the core elements of the conflict trigger. By doing so, we honor the employee's voice and provide them with an opportunity to gain clarity about root causes and motivations driving the conflict.

- What was the trigger(s)?
- What caused the person to seek help? Specifically, what happened at that moment that prompted the request?

While we provide you as the HR professional clarity for what we are targeting in the section by using the commonly used conflict term "trigger," we recognize the sensitivity surrounding this term, as it may evoke distress or discomfort for some individuals. We encourage you to explore alternative terminology that better resonates with your experiences and preferences. Alternative words might be "catalyst," "precursor," or "prompt." Your question could simply be: "What specific event or circumstance led to you feeling upset or angry?"

R—REACTION

Having read or heard so many post-conflict discussions, it is clear to us that this is the most skipped part of the note-taking process. What was done and what is being done?

- What was the employee's immediate reaction? What did he or she specifically do, think, and feel immediately after being triggered?

- What were the employee's first actions after that? Did they file a report, seek a mentor, or tell a friend?
- Besides visiting the manager, what other actions have been put into play?
- Who else has the employee talked to about this matter (coworkers, friends, mentor)? As an example, when an employee says their mentor encouraged them to seek HR help, the note might be "mentor encouraged HR visit."

Even seemingly mundane details can hold significant relevance in the context of conflict resolution. This reaction can be as simple as the employee asking another employee for a meeting, which is where a disclosure that a formal complaint process has been engaged is captured.

It's also important to recognize the limitations of our HR role at this stage of the process. While immediate action may be necessary in emergency situations, such as instances of harassment or safety concerns, in most cases HR professionals must refrain from offering recommendations or solutions until the intake process is complete. This allows the intake notes to serve as a pure and unadulterated account of the employee's concerns and experiences, free from the influence of external perspectives or expert opinions.

T—THOUGHTS

At the core of our humanity lies our capacity for complex thought and reasoning. As beings endowed with high-level cognitive abilities, humans possess a natural inclination to make sense of the world around them, often through the creation of narratives or stories. These stories serve as cognitive constructs that help individuals process and interpret their experiences, providing a framework through which events are understood and contextualized. These narratives can sometimes become deeply ingrained in individuals' minds, evolving into entrenched thoughts that shape their perceptions and responses to conflict.

The ability to discern between these internal narratives and objectively supportable facts is invaluable. By distinguishing between subjective interpretations and objective realities, HR professionals can glean valuable insights into the underlying dynamics of the conflict and identify potential points of resolution. Documenting these narratives as they are initially recounted provides a valuable record that can inform subsequent discussions and interventions.

It's essential to recognize that by the time employees seek assistance from their managers or HR they may have already confided in others, such as trusted friends, family members, or colleagues. These external conversations can influence and shape the narrative surrounding the conflict, potentially leading to the distortion or exaggeration of facts. As HR professionals, we play an essential role in helping untangle and clarify these narratives, guiding employees toward a more objective understanding of the situation.

By acknowledging and addressing the influence of these external conversations and internal narratives, HR professionals can foster a more transparent and constructive dialogue with employees. Through attentive listening and thoughtful documentation, we can help to separate fact from fiction, paving the way for more effective conflict resolution and a greater sense of clarity for all involved. Your own thoughts might be—

- Different than what is supportable, what does the employee think is happening?

- What does the employee think the other person(s) is doing, and why?

- What does the employee believe to be true, but does not have evidence for?

E—EMOTIONS

In this pivotal section, clarity emerges as emotions come to the forefront. Far too frequently, HR professionals and managers inadvertently perpetuate misunderstandings by assuming and relaying inaccurate assessments of an employee's emotional state. HR professionals must attune their ears to nuanced expressions such as feeling disrespected, embarrassed, angry, or hurt. In doing so, we are positioned not only to empathize but also to de-escalate tensions, preventing conflicts from spiraling out of control from the employee's perspective. It is also essential to discern between feelings and thoughts expressed by the employee. Phrases like "I feel like we should . . ." may indicate a thought rather than a genuine emotion, and should be documented accordingly. This section serves as a receptacle for uncertainties and complexities, where statements such as "I don't know how I feel about this" find their place. By honing our ability to discern and document emotions accurately, we pave the way for more nuanced and effective conflict resolution strategies. Questions to consider are—

- Aside from the immediate reaction and feelings, how does the employee feel now?
- Does the employee have a perspective on the other person's emotions?
- Does the employee feel like there is no hope of resolving this conflict (even using a word like "desperate")?

D—DESIRES

Employees often become deeply entrenched in narrating their version of events during conflicts, to the extent that they may not have clarity regarding what constitutes an acceptable resolution. This lack of clarity can hinder progress in resolving the conflict effectively. In some instances, the comments shared during intake discussions may appear unrealistic or improbable from the perspective of HR professionals, yet they remain significant and should be duly noted. Even seemingly implausible comments may provide valuable insights into the employee's mindset, motivations, and underlying concerns, which, if left unexplored, could exacerbate the conflict. As HR professionals, we have the opportunity to initiate forward-leaning processes by approaching these thoughts with a gentle and curious demeanor, especially when documenting them. By demonstrating genuine interest and curiosity in understanding the employee's perspective, we create an environment conducive to uncovering hidden motivations, unearthing potential solutions, and ultimately fostering a more constructive dialogue. This approach not only enriches our understanding of the conflict but also lays the groundwork for collaborative problem-solving and the identification of mutually acceptable outcomes. Embracing a mindset of curiosity and openness when engaging with employees is key, even when their comments may initially appear far-fetched or incongruous. Questions you may have include—

- Going back to when the employee brought this to you, what was that goal(s)?
- What does the employee want to happen now (catharsis already happening by just telling you this story)?

- What would make this person feel whole again? From the employee's perspective, what does a fix look like?

- Maybe the employee is already moving past the point of the pain or concern, so what is possible now from their perspective?

As HR professionals, one of the most valuable contributions we can offer employees navigating conflict is our ability to assist them in distilling and organizing the myriad details that often seem overwhelming and difficult to track. The anecdote at the chapter's start highlights how Ben could have communicated more clearly by providing a SORTED summary of the original dialogue. This structured approach would also have allowed Thomas, as the HR representative using the SORTED framework, to ask clarifying questions without seeming investigative, fostering an informative intake conversation. The SORTED model serves as a guiding light, leading us and the employees we support toward realistic and manageable next steps by systematically dissecting and examining these details. It is essential for HR professionals to adopt a stance that prioritizes thoughtful consideration over hasty action, recognizing that rushing toward a resolution may not always be feasible or conducive to sustainable outcomes. In instances where immediate action is not warranted it is perfectly acceptable to express this to the employee, affirming their input and proposing a collaborative approach to determining the way forward. This might involve scheduling a follow-up meeting to co-create a plan of action or seeking guidance from higher leadership, all while maintaining transparency and partnership with the employee.

Critical Thinking Questions

1. How could you benefit from creating a consistent note-taking process when engaging in conflict discussions?

2. Which parts of the SORTED model are new to you, and how might they help you in navigating complex situations more adeptly?

3. In what ways can you tailor and augment each component of the model to better suit your unique approach and organizational context?

Invitational Mediation Techniques

Jill, the HR specialist for a large firm, is approached by two leaders of sister organizations. These organizations are code-pendent, with one focusing on the beginning of the process and the other dealing with the output. Each has rather large teams, built over many years by valuable technical experts. The two leaders tell Jill that two key members, Frank and Hope, one from each organization, will no longer work together, and this is having a major impact on a very important project. The leaders describe being in shock, since the employees have worked on several key projects together and are known to be friends. These leaders are hoping Jill can help by meeting with the employees. Jill has some idea of formal mediation from the perspective of resolving formal grievances, so she wonders whether a media-tion process is what is needed. Her next thought is that maybe she isn't the right person to bring the two employees together to find a way forward because it seems so complicated, and she wonders whether she should just outsource the problem to a trained expert mediator.

In the fast-paced realm of workplace dynamics, mediation emerges as a pivotal process aimed at reducing the cost of unproductive conflicts and fostering constructive communication channels. At its essence, mediation unfolds as a collaborative endeavor, facilitated by an impartial third-party figure, often a proficient HR specialist adept at navigating interpersonal complexities. This intervention serves as a conduit, drawing together disputing parties ensnared in communication impasses. The overarching objective is to engender a conducive environment where dialogues can unfold, thereby mitigating the ramifications of disputes on the workplace fabric, and to instill a proactive organizational ethos that prioritizes early intervention in conflicts.

Traditionally, the purview of mediation has been predominantly tethered to the resolution of formally articulated grievances, reflective of a prevailing legalistic paradigm entrenched within HR frameworks. The evolution of mediation practice, underscored by professional training, heralds a departure from such narrow confines. As seasoned mediators imbued with a comprehensive understanding of mediation principles and standards—confidentiality, neutrality, and self-determination among them—we recognize the inherent efficacy and effectiveness of mediation methodologies, transcending mere procedural adherence. Our epiphany is realizing that the very techniques we employ in mediating disputes informally frequently mirror established mediation protocols.

Armed with this insight, we invite you to participate on a journey toward institutionalizing mediation practices within the workplace as an early intervention tactic, thereby fostering a culture of proactive conflict resolution. By harmonizing formal mediation tenets with everyday workplace interactions, we endeavor to cultivate a workplace culture characterized by transparency, equity, and constructive engagement. In doing so we not only mitigate the disruptive impact of conflicts, but also nurture a strong organizational framework that is resilient to the ebbs and flows of interpersonal disputes.

Have you ever wondered if the internal HR department needs to involve an external mediator who's formally trained? What did HR professionals do before mediation was handled by experts? Traditionally, HR has been proactive in managing workplace disputes alongside company leadership. While mediation is recognized as valuable beyond workplaces and across borders, its implementation varies. Our aim is to simplify the process, making it a practical intervention strategy for issues not requiring formal procedures like EEO or grievance protocols. For disputes needing settlements, typically started through formal processes, we recommend extensive mediation training, usually spanning 40 hours or more. Our mediation strategy complements rather than replaces skilled mediators, especially for complex legal conflicts. Early involvement of neutral third parties shows promise in reducing formal mediations and workplace conflicts. It's time to effectively utilize mediation methods for your benefit.

We're offering a practical alternative to the traditional legalistic approach to mediation: a tried-and-tested restorative conversation process designed to empower HR specialists like Jill in our opening anecdote to swiftly and confidently address issues. We call it the invitational mediation method, and it is a combination of facilitative and narrative mediation styles. In a facilitative mediation style, the mediator primarily facilitates communication and negotiation between the parties. The mediator helps the parties identify issues, explore interests, and generate options for resolution. The facilitative mediator does not offer opinions or solutions, but assists the parties in reaching their own agreements. In narrative mediation styles, the process emphasizes storytelling as a means of understanding and resolving conflicts. The parties are encouraged to share their narratives, perspectives, and experiences related to the dispute. The mediator helps the parties explore alternative narratives and create a shared story that can lead to a mutually acceptable resolution.

In invitational mediation, instead of having a solution mindset for the meeting, our approach invites parties to share their stories, respect each other's perspectives, engage in dialogue, and collaboratively devise a way forward. While we acknowledge the importance of solutions and objectives in mediation for resolving business issues, we prioritize setting the stage for ongoing success in the participants' relationship beyond the immediate problem. In the invitational mediation model, the HR professional or a leader guided by HR acts as a facilitator, allowing the parties to generate solutions themselves and feel empowered in shaping the future direction of their relationship.

Without sugar-coating the situation, we need to address a concerning trend we've observed regarding growing frustrations in the workplace. While the causes may vary—whether it's related to politics, post-COVID effects, or mental health—it's unproductive to dwell too much on unraveling these complexities when immediate interventions are needed. HR is facing overwhelming demands, and many root issues are beyond our direct control.

Despite our efforts to keep this book practical rather than overly theoretical, it's worth considering the perceived organizational support theory, which suggests that employees feel more supported when processes like mediation and conflict coaching are in place, even if they don't directly use these services.[4] Productivity thrives in supportive environments, and HR plays an important role in ensuring the provision of necessary services. Employees desire an environment where ideas can be freely exchanged, but this can sometimes escalate into challenging conflicts. HR professionals must rely on fundamental skills and established processes and be readily available during times of conflict, which can be professionally vulnerable moments for employees. Even if successful restorative conversations

----
4   R. Eisenberger and F. Stinglhamber, *Perceived Organizational Support: Fostering Enthusiastic and Productive Employees* (Washington, DC: American Psychological Association, 2011).

are sometimes challenging, they may still allow you to find satisfaction in your HR role. Most HR professionals enjoy problem-solving, and seeing the positive impact of our interventions is rewarding. So take pride in actively addressing these workplace conflicts rather than merely observing them.

The Intake Process

Respectful conversations serve as invitations for mediation. Instances where mediation techniques may be necessary can be identified by HR leaders, by one of the parties in the conflict, or by HR itself upon becoming aware of a concern. Regardless of the initiator, HR professionals, as leaders within the organization, always commence mediation with clear objectives:

1. *Establish boundaries on confidentiality guarantees.* HR acknowledges that when individuals seek assistance from HR, they are involving the organization. HR cannot promise complete confidentiality as the aim is to facilitate progress, which may mean involving others as necessary. HR assures transparency and regular communication regarding the next steps in addressing the concern.

2. *Clarify business impact.* It is important to focus on the business implications of conflict while addressing interpersonal issues. HR plays a key role in engaging with leadership to understand how the conflict affects the

organization's operations. By assessing disruptions to work, considering the involvement of other employees, and defining post-mediation success criteria, HR ensures that the mediation process is aligned with specific impacts on the business.

The mediator anchors the mediation by crafting problem opportunity statements. These statements are concise, highlighting business impacts without assigning blame. They serve as a guidepost for achieving the primary mediation goal. While mediations can evolve to address multiple goals, these statements act as a minimum outcome to strive for:

- *A mediation between two department leaders.* "The ongoing disagreement between (name the two departments) over shared resources is hindering collaboration and productivity, causing project delays, and lowering employee morale. Resolving this conflict is essential for meeting [Project XYZ] milestones."

- *A mediation between technical subject matter experts.* "Recent technological challenges have disrupted day-to-day operations, highlighted by a debate during the XYZ business partner meeting that led to an abrupt end without a project plan. Let's collaborate to address these challenges for smoother workflows and reduced disruptions."

- *A mediation between two team members with inter-connected team roles.* "A communication breakdown between [sales employee] and [marketing employee] is causing inefficiencies, missed opportunities, and delays in implementing a communication plan targeting our customers. During this mediation, we will look for the cause and brainstorm solutions for a more effective way forward."

These problem opportunity statements are clear, neutral, concise, actionable, and measurable. They guide parties toward communicating their desired outcomes post-mediation.

- *Set expectations with leaders.* The mediator emphasizes to leaders that the goal of restorative conversations is to restore working relationships and address business impacts, not to disclose private discussions. HR helps leaders understand the boundaries of confidentiality and encourages them to focus on outcomes rather than details upon the participants' return to work. The mediator assists parties in agreeing on task-based, outcome-focused statements, which may require approval from leaders not involved in the mediation process.

Mediators also need to remain impartial and consider all input information, regardless of whether it comes from leaders or parties involved in the conflict. While leaders provide valuable perspectives on business problems, it's essential not to lean into problem-solving discussions or mediation decisions until all relevant information has been gathered.

The Pre-Mediation Caucus

Before the formal mediation session begins, it's essential to conduct a private preparatory meeting with each participant—a pre-mediation caucus. This initial meeting typically lasts about 30 minutes and involves several key steps and objectives:

1. *Assessing the situation.* The mediator uses this time to ensure there are no underlying issues that might affect the mediation process. Participants may disclose pertinent information such as ongoing legal cases, medical conditions, job changes, or other factors that could impact the mediation's effectiveness.

2. *Explaining the process.* The mediator clarifies their role as a neutral facilitator and outlines the mediation process. This includes discussing the purpose of mediation, emphasizing impartiality, and highlighting the collaborative nature of finding solutions.

3. *Scheduling and confidentiality.* The mediator sends calendar invites for the preliminary meeting and stresses the importance of confidentiality within the company's normal business practices. HR may remind participants

of the goal to foster open dialogue while ensuring mediation is the appropriate step forward. When sending calendar invites as a mediator you need to prioritize confidentiality, especially when utilizing shared calendars. To uphold the integrity of the mediation process and respect the privacy of all involved parties, consider describing the event simply as an "appointment" without divulging specific details. This practice ensures that sensitive information remains protected and prevents unintentional disclosures. By maintaining discretion in calendar invitations, mediators demonstrate their commitment to fostering a safe and confidential environment for constructive dialogue and resolution.

4. *Setting expectations for the mediation session.* Participants are informed about the business rules for the upcoming mediation session, including the opportunity for each party to share their perspective without interruptions. They are encouraged to consider their goals for the meeting and imagine the other party's objectives. The mediator may ask both parties to privately complete a perspective-seeking worksheet as homework before the mediation event (see example worksheet in the Appendix). Statements for business rules might include—

- *Respect.* "Please treat each other with courtesy and respect. Let's listen attentively and refrain from interrupting while others are speaking."

- *Confidentiality.* "What is discussed in these sessions remains confidential. Please refrain from sharing any information outside of our discussion. This is especially important for not only honest conversation between you, but also for the reputation of mediation in the workplace. We want all of our employees to feel like this is a special space for rich dialogue without fear of gossip."

- *Voluntary participation.* "Participation is voluntary. If we need a break or feel uncomfortable, please feel free to tell me."

- *Honesty and transparency.* "Let's strive for honesty and transparency in our communication. This will facilitate trust and constructive dialogue."

- *One speaker at a time.* "To ensure effective communication, let's allow one person to speak at a time and avoid talking over each other."

- *Stay solution-focused.* "Let's work together to identify solutions on possible ways forward. Let's raise current perspectives, but not dwell on past issues since mediation is a forward-leaning process."

It's common for employees to want to contribute additional business rules. When they bring these up, it's important to listen attentively and take note of the insights they provide you as mediator. For instance, if a rule regarding mutual respect for time is suggested, it could indicate that one party feels their time is being disregarded or that they perceive the mediation process as unproductive. While these remarks should be regarded as informational rather than accusatory, they can offer valuable input for crafting language that addresses the needs of both parties.

Although these business rules might have been mentioned previously in preliminary sessions, often laden with emotional nuances and blame attribution, your role is to guide their formal agreement during the joint session. Here are some common topics that might emerge during discussions with employees in preliminary sessions:

- *Mutual respect for time.* "I'd like us to agree to be respectful of my time and keep our discussions focused on the business issues."

- *Positive language.* "I'd like us to use positive and constructive language toward me."

- *Accountability.* "I'd like us to be accountable to our own actions."

- *Gratitude.* "I think we should express appreciation for each other's work and contributions in this mediation session."

- *Confidentiality and technology guidelines.* "This meeting will not be recorded, and all notes will be destroyed after the session."

- *Contingency plans for remote meetings.* "In case of technological issues, here is the number to call, and all conversation will stop until we are reunited. In addition, please ensure you are in a private location to avoid being overheard."

- *Confirmation of meetings with other party.* "I will be meeting with (name of the other party)" or "I have already met with (name of the other party)."

- *Establishing meeting logistics.* "Here are a few logistical details for our meeting (state the neutral meeting location, three-hour or more duration depending on complexity, and behavioral norms)." Are there any additional logistical needs or preferences you need to make?

- *Emphasizing voluntary participation.* "Attendance is voluntary." HR addresses any concerns about "voluntold" participation and reassures participants of the goal to address the business impact of the dispute collaboratively. When business conflicts arise, simply allowing the conflicts to continue unresolved is not a reasonable option. You may have to discuss the benefits by saying, "The key benefit of invitational mediation is that it emphasizes the opportunity for both parties to actively collaborate in creating mutually agreeable outcomes rather than having an outside third party dictate the resolution. In this way the parties can co-create a solution that meets both of your needs and interests so that you have ownership over the way forward."

- *Preparation and follow-up.* "As you prepare for the upcoming session, it is helpful to think of a few goals you have for the session. I will be following up with you in a joint email offering three available days and times."

The Power of the Apology

Apologies hold immense power in the mediation process. Mediators can play a crucial role in facilitating and guiding the parties toward meaningful apologies that can help resolve conflicts and repair relationships. Things to keep in mind about the nuances involved in apologies—and your role as an HR professional—include the following:

HR TIP: The mediator picks three dates/times after learning about any upcoming planned absences and offers them in a follow-up joint email. For efficiency, participants are told to reply to all with which of the three, if any, would not work on their schedule.

- *Consider context.* Apologies can have different meanings and significance across various cultures. In some cultures an apology is seen as an admission of fault, while in others it is a sincere expression of sorrow and empathy, regardless of who is at fault. Some cultures prefer public apologies as a way to repair reputations, while others may find private apologies more appropriate.

- *Validate the need.* As a mediator, you can acknowledge the need for an apology, even though we don't personally directly ask one party to apologize. This can be done in the preliminary meeting or during the mediation event itself. By saying something like "I hear your need for an apology, and I think we need to discuss this further to understand how it could help," you are validating the offended party's feelings and creating an opportunity for open discussion.

- *Set the stage.* In your opening remarks for the mediation event, you can set the stage for apologies by stating that the mediation may involve the desire to issue an apology on one or more topics. Explain the importance of emotions in the mediation process and how a sincere apology can demonstrate empathy and perspective taking.

- *Invite reflection.* If one party expresses a need for an apology but none is offered, and the mediation seems stuck, you can ask both parties to reflect on things they would and should have done differently. This can lead to one or both parties acknowledging their mistakes, which can then open the door for a meaningful apology.

Remember, as a mediator, you are not asking one party to apologize directly, as that could be perceived as aligning with one participant over the other. Instead, you are creating a safe and supportive environment where the parties can explore the power of apology and its potential to resolve the conflict. By understanding the cultural nuances of apologies, acknowledging the need for them, encouraging them in your opening remarks, and facilitating reflection and acknowledgment of mistakes, you can help the parties navigate this delicate but powerful aspect of the mediation process.

The Joint Session

The mindset of the joint session in an invitational mediation session is to invite each party to share their perspective and to hear each other's perspective. The mediation process previously outlined involves several key steps and strategies to facilitate productive dialogue and resolution between the parties involved. Here's a clearer breakdown of each component:

Joint session opening:

1. The mediator sets the tone by emphasizing the goal of understanding each other's perspectives.

2. Because each party has a unique perspective on how the conflict began and what the current situation looks like,

an archaeological dig or similar metaphor can be helpful. Explain that conflict resolution is similar to archaeologists starting their excavations at different points on a site. As the archaeologists dig, each layer reveals more about what is underneath—in this case the parties' positions, interests, and underlying needs. Parties are encouraged to "dig" into each other's viewpoints with curiosity starting at the surface with the surface-level "artifacts" like their positions: what they think happened. Dig down to priorities for resolving the conflict. Then move deeper down to what seems to be stuck. This process involves describing their own layers and exploring the other layers and they are reminded that because they are at the same archaeology site, there are likely many things in common that can be uncovered.

3. Parties are encouraged to share their stories without pressure to abandon their perspectives.

4. The mediator reassures parties about confidentiality and the neutral role of the mediator.

Conducting the session:

1. The mediator prompts one party to speak while ensuring the other listens without interruption. Dialogue between the parties ensues only after the uninterrupted opening statements.

2. Parties are encouraged to take brief notes for further discussion. These notes will be destroyed by the mediator.

3. The mediator takes notes on key points and observes nonverbal cues to guide the conversation. These notes are also destroyed by the mediator.

4. Reframing techniques are used to shift the focus or energy of the discussion when necessary. For example, if the thread is on "feeling disrespected" without much progress, the mediator would ask the parties to explore what "feeling respected" would look like to each of them.

Questioning techniques:

1. During times of heightened tension during the conversation, the mediator owns the responsibility to help bring clarity by slowing the pace of the room by asking open-ended questions. The mediator's goal when asking questions is to encourage further dialogue without appearing to investigate.

2. Silence is allowed to facilitate reflection and expression.

3. Questions are asked with patience, allowing for natural responses and additional insights.

Managing emotions:

1. The mediator reframes emotional moments as opportunities for exploration rather than conflict.

2. Parties are prompted to express their feelings and perspectives in response to each other's statements.

3. Progress toward resolution is acknowledged, particularly when discussions shift toward future possibilities.

Example Mediator Opening Remarks

Modify and create your own statement, and ensure it is reviewed by your legal counsel so that it can be consistent with your organization and locality law needs.

"Good morning/afternoon, [Name of parties]. Welcome to this mediation session. I am [Name], your mediator today. I want to emphasize my role as an impartial mediator in this process. My goal is not to take sides or favor any party, but rather to facilitate a fair and productive conversation. I am here to ensure that each party feels heard and respected throughout our discussion. Your trust in my neutrality is essential for the success of this mediation. My role as mediator is to manage the process we will

continued

use today, and I have a few opening remarks to ensure we start off clear about our process.

[If virtual] Before we begin, I want to emphasize the use of technology in our communication today. In the event of a technical issue, please call [number] for assistance. Our conversation will stop until all parties are present.

Throughout this session, I encourage respectful listening. Each of you has a unique perspective, and it's vital that we hear and attempt to understand each other's viewpoints to move forward. Let's envision our dialogue as an archaeological dig, where each party has a unique perspective on the site. As archaeologists, we'll start our excavation at different points, but as we dig deeper, each layer reveals more about what lies underneath—your positions, interests, and underlying needs. I encourage you to "dig" into each other's viewpoints with curiosity, starting at the surface with the surface-level "artifacts" like your positions: in other words, what you think happened. Then we'll dig down to your priorities and move deeper to uncover what seems to be stuck.

Take time to the tell the other party the full story behind this conflict, including any nuances of your perspective that may not be known. You will be uninterrupted by the other party during the opening remarks. Remember, there's no pressure to abandon your own perspective during these uninterrupted opening remarks. We are here to listen and understand before we make any decisions on the way forward.

Throughout, you can expect me to ask open-ended, non-investigatory questions as needed to facilitate dialogue or help us reframe something we might be stuck on. I will also slow us down when needed to encourage reflection. We are not in a rush today.

This session is confidential. While I encourage you to take notes to aid your active listening, as I will as well, these notes will be destroyed at the end of our discussion. Also, there will be no recording of our conversation. The only enduring document will be the notes I take and share with the both of you about our agreement on the way forward. We will co-create this way forward in our session today.

Do you have any questions for me and do you agree with our way forward? [pause]

Let's begin our journey now toward understanding and resolution. I believe we are here today to discuss this problem opportunity statement about [state it]. [Name], I invite you to begin."

Breakthrough phase:

1. The mediator announces and congratulates progress toward collaborative problem-solving without rushing closure.

2. Emotional outbursts may occur as parties prepare for closure and adjust to the collaborative process, signaling ongoing engagement with the mediator is necessary. Mediators are aware that practicing debate with the help of a dialogue facilitator about future-oriented goals is helpful for future workplace interactions after the mediation.

The mediation process aims to create a safe and constructive environment for parties to explore their perspectives, communicate effectively, and work toward mutually beneficial solutions.

Insider Tips

We'd be remiss if we didn't provide you with a few insider HR tips for mediating. Here are some we consider key to success during the process:

Focused listening:

1. While the parties speak, subtly shift your gaze to the listener to gauge their reaction. This encourages direct communication between the parties and helps you interpret nonverbal cues from the receiver of the information.

2. Body language is cultural and differs—but the brief, immediate emotional human reactions are universal, so you don't want to miss seeing them.

Realistic optimism:

1. Maintain a positive outlook on the parties' ability to find common ground.

2. Your optimism influences the atmosphere in the room and motivates parties toward collaboration.

Environmental considerations:

1. In virtual mediations, ensure both parties are positioned at a similar distance from the camera for balanced visibility.

2. In physical settings, choose an intimate room with the mediator positioned at the head of the table for optimal engagement.

Commencing the process:

1. Begin the mediation only when both parties are present.

2. In physical sessions, ensure both parties are invited to enter the room together.

3. In virtual sessions, utilize a waiting room feature to avoid one-sided interactions before the mediation starts.

These tips emphasize the importance of attentive listening, fostering a positive atmosphere, creating balanced environments, and ensuring equal participation from both parties at the outset of the mediation event.

Closure

As the parties move toward the conclusion of the mediation event, it's time to navigate the path ahead and establish resolutions—an invitation to the future. Before delving into decision-making processes, it's important to embrace a nuanced understanding of fairness. While fairness is a term often mentioned in mediation, its definition varies for each participant. As mediators, we adopt a neutral stance on this notion, recognizing that fairness primarily pertains to the integrity of the process itself. Before initiating closure, ask yourself the following questions:

1. Have we ensured that all parties are well-informed about the mediation process and its aim for constructive outcomes?

2. Have we explicitly signaled the transition into the closure phase, inviting any remaining concerns to be voiced and addressed?

3. Have we outlined the decision-making process to maintain inclusivity and ensure each party's voice is upheld? This entails the mediator drafting outcomes, reading them aloud, ensuring behavioral specificity without stating fault, and seeking explicit agreement from all involved on wording and intent.

4. Have we privately discussed the voluntary nature of mediation with both parties during preliminary meetings?

5. Have we facilitated uninterrupted opening statements and provided ample opportunity for each participant to express themselves during the meetings, thereby preventing one party from dominating the conversation? While it's important to allow employees to speak for themselves, actively inviting input and balancing the dialogue ensures a fairer exchange of perspectives.

When HR assumes the role of fostering fairness within the mediation process in these ways, it is far more likely to be successful.

Introduction and transition:

1. Start by thanking all participants for their commitment and efforts throughout the session.

2. Inform them that it's time to move into the next stage, which involves documenting the outcomes and actions agreed upon.

Role of the scribe:

1. Explain the role of the scribe (usually the mediator to increase perception of a fair recording) in accurately documenting the agreed-upon statements.

2. Emphasize the importance of rewriting and rereading statements to ensure accuracy.

3. Clarify the criteria for outcome statements:

    •   They should be behaviorally specific, detailing tasks, deadlines, and review points.

    •   Avoid assigning blame or documenting apologies.

4. Format them akin to staff meeting notes. If you believe you need a formal signed settlement document, you should consult with your general counsel or attorney about a formal mediation process and perhaps secure a formally trained mediator. In the invitational mediation model, the outcome statements are not formal or signed documents, but are mediated intention summaries.

5. Cover both task-oriented and relationship-building activities.

Addressing differences:

1. Acknowledge that decision-making often involves differing perspectives.

2. Encourage participants to utilize their mediation alliances to navigate disagreements respectfully.

3. Recommend a structured approach to resolving differences:

- Encourage active listening and acknowledgment of positive aspects of each other's ideas ("What I like about that idea is . . . and . . . ")

- Facilitate a discussion using tools like Venn diagrams to visualize areas of agreement and disagreement.

4. Ensure participants feel respected by documenting their contributions.

Resolving persistent differences:

1. If disagreements persist, the mediator leads a discussion on perspective seeking.

2. Facilitate a pros and cons dialogue for each possibility.

3. Encourage participants to articulate their perspectives on the proposed outcomes.

4. Emphasize the importance of avoiding hasty compromises that may lead to future issues.

5. Incorporate periodic review dates into outcome statements to allow for adjustments.

Documentation and confidentiality:

1. Stress the confidentiality of sessions notes, which will be destroyed by the mediator except for agreed-upon outcomes.

2. Facilitate a discussion on what information can be shared upon returning to regular sessions.

3. Advise participants on handling inquiries from leaders or others, suggesting a simple response to maintain confidentiality. An example like "We had a good conversation with a few outcomes we agreed to work on together" will suffice and help the parties not get caught off guard.

4. Tell the participants you will type and send one email with the agreed-upon outcomes to both participants. Lead a discussion about how they will jointly present those outcomes to the appropriate organizational leader.

In this phase, try using AI to help with brainstorming. AI can play several roles in assisting with mediations, offering valuable support to mediators, the parties involved, and the overall process:

1. *Data analysis.* AI can analyze large volumes of legal documents, case law, and precedent to provide insights into potential outcomes and strategies. This analysis can help parties understand their positions better and make informed decisions during negotiations.

2. *Predictive analytics.* By analyzing past mediation cases and outcomes, AI can provide predictions on the likely resolution of a current dispute. This helps parties manage

their expectations and make more informed decisions about settlement offers.

3. *Crafting clearer outcome statements.* Technologies can assist in summarizing and extracting key points from legal documents, emails, and other communication between parties. This helps mediators focus on relevant information and identify common ground more efficiently.

4. *Communication support.* AI chatbots or virtual assistants can provide parties with information, answer common questions, and facilitate communication during the mediation process. This can help parties feel more informed and supported throughout the proceedings. Employees might even perceive these tools to be less biased than ideas brought forward from either party or you as the mediator.

5. *Online dispute resolution.* AI-powered platforms can facilitate online mediation sessions, offering features such as secure communication channels, document sharing, and real-time collaboration tools. This enables parties to participate in mediations remotely, reducing logistical barriers and increasing accessibility. These technologies can enhance the security and confidentiality of mediation notes and outcome statements.

As early adopters, we've found AI has the potential to enhance various aspects of the mediation process, from data analysis and communication support to decision-making and conflict resolution—ultimately contributing to more efficient and effective dispute resolution outcomes.

Let's revisit the mediation session involving Frank and Hope from the case study that opened this chapter. It emerged that both Frank and Hope were candidates for promotion during this cycle. Frank suspected that Hope was deliberately withholding crucial information regarding an important project to enhance her chances of promotion. To his dismay, Frank learned from his boss that Hope's leader had advised her to adopt such tactics. This revelation was particularly shocking to Frank because over the years, Hope had become not just a colleague but also a trusted friend.

Frank's boss advised him on how to handle the situation by withholding information that could potentially give Hope an advantage over him. Through the mediation discussions, both Frank and Hope came to realize that their bosses were engaged in a competition for limited promotion opportunities. It became apparent that securing a promotion within their respective teams would enhance their bosses' resumes. As a result of the mediation, several outcomes were swiftly outlined:

1. Frank and Hope agreed to let the project's needs override either of their wants for promotion.

2. Frank and Hope agreed that when they heard something that was contradictory to how they both knew each other to behave, they would text the other with the word "strange," which would signal the need for a private

meeting at the coffee shop to discuss it. Both agreed to prioritize these meetings.

3. When we asked AI to rewrite and clarify this mediation outcome statement, we immediately received this back:

Frank and Hope have reached an agreement to prioritize the project's requirements over their individual desires for promotion.

Additionally, they have established a communication protocol: if either party observes behavior from the other that contradicts their usual conduct, they will send a text message containing the word "strange." This will serve as a signal for arranging a private meeting at the coffee shop to address the issue. Both parties have committed to giving these meetings precedence on their individual calendars.

The revised version is indeed clearer, but stays consistent with our intent and tone. As another example, if we were to request a statement regarding an agreement a leader offers to an employee to mentor and facilitate the training and advancement of their employee, we might say "Ms. Bagley, as Tom's supervisor, agrees to mentor Tom and support him for the external XYZ leadership development program." When we tasked AI with rephrasing and elaborating on this statement, it makes it clearer, but still maintains a nonlegalistic tone suitable for a workplace agreement:

Ms. Bagley, in her capacity as Tom's supervisor, commits to providing ongoing mentoring and support to Tom as he pursues enrollment in the external XYZ leadership development program. This mentoring will occur on a bi-weekly basis, with structured sessions aimed at addressing Tom's professional growth and development needs.

Ms. Bagley will take responsibility for initiating invitations for these mentoring sessions, ensuring regularity and consistency in their occurrence. Should the XYZ leadership development program not be available or if Tom does not meet the qualifications for enrollment, Ms. Bagley pledges to explore alternative development opportunities or resources to support Tom's career advancement aspirations.

Additionally, in the event that circumstances arise which hinder the participation of either party in the agreed-upon mentoring arrangement, both Ms. Bagley and Tom agree to communicate openly and promptly to address any concerns and seek mutually agreeable solutions to maintain progress toward Tom's career goals.

When crafting your outcome statements, think about the tone you want to express. You can opt for a relaxed and informal style akin to meeting notes, or a more formal tone suitable for performance planning documents. Ensure consistency through-out, and consult your legal advisors, who are adept at drafting such statements.

It's natural to consider what happens if both parties are unable to reach an agreement. In anticipation of this scenario—which is actually quite rare—we pose a crucial question to the parties: "If agreement seems unattainable, what do you anticipate will be the most likely outcome when you return to the workplace?" The mediator documents the responses for both parties to see and contribute to, and acknowledges the consequences of reaching an impasse. The mediator encourages the parties for a final time, and if no resolution is found, offers the option of a second mediation session within the next day or two, if feasible. It is rare that a workplace conflict mediation results in no way forward, but when it happens, the leader and HR have done all they can do and a different process is needed.

If indeed the mediator has tried everything, HR does what HR must do and works with the leaders through employee relations efforts. In this case, you do honor the confidentiality alliance and simply refer back to leadership as not resolved without any "fault" discussion. We recommend you wait a day or two to allow the parties to sleep on it, because sometimes a party wants to try again after thinking it through.

We end the most challenging mediations that seem to have not progressed by stating: "It is clear that we have not made the progress we hoped today. I'll get back to leadership to decide what can be done about the business problem and I'll do so without a discussion about fault. As I do this, I'd like to offer that either of you can call me within the next few days and ask me to invite the other employee back to another session, and I'd be happy to continue our work."

We've included a summary checklist in the Appendix to help you get started—but we consider this chapter a foundation upon which to construct your personalized mediation checklist. Crafting such a reference document will not only bolster your consistency and confidence, but also enhance your credibility as an esteemed HR professional.

Critical Thinking Questions

1. Write your introductory message that you will deliver during the joint session. Considering the concept of an archaeological dig analogy, is there an alternative metaphor or approach that may better resonate with your team?

2. Which open-ended questions will you integrate into your standard practice for joint sessions? Record these inquiries on your checklist for easy reference.

3. In your preliminary meetings with employees to gather perspectives, how will you incorporate the elements of HERE introduced in a previous chapter? Specifically,

which aspects of HERE will you emphasize to ensure a comprehensive understanding of their viewpoints?

4. What will you add to your own standard business rules for the session?

Mediating Team Troubles

Avery continues to see churn on her project team. It feels like every month someone is leaving to take a new position, and Avery learns through trusted sources that others are looking too. At a loss, she asks HR to do a few exit interviews and discovers that there is competition, gossip, and knowledge hoarding on the team. With HR's encouragement, Avery thinks the team just needs to take a break for a team-building exercise, and they're determined to make it a good one. Finding an expert facilitator and an ideal location for an entire day, Avery is all set to turn this team trouble around. Avery tells the facilitator the results of the exit interviews and is assured that a commonly used assessment to show different styles of working together, and a team intervention that encourages fun problem-solving together, is exactly what the team needs. Avery doesn't agree completely, and encourages a breakout session where team members can feel free to voice concerns. The facilitator suggests that this activity should be the last thing on the agenda, because earlier work in the day will build the trust necessary for honest communication. The facilitator also encourages the leader to not take part in this activity so that employees will feel freer to express concerns. The day seems to go fine, and the facilitator provides a brainstorming activity at the end of the day where a list of ideas for improvement (or is it complaints?) is collected, as promised. The next day, Avery thanks the team for their input and promises the group they can work on the problems. Avery takes the facilitator's advice and personally picks a few quick wins to implement and communicate to show good faith. Who knew getting a second coffee pot and implementing a choice for 10-hour, four-day workweeks was the source of all the team's troubles and could make this type of difference? The rest of the ideas are sorted and distributed to small groups with due dates. Avery feels confident that the churn will now stop. About a month later, two more employees resign. The exit interviews show the same concerns, except both also say that a "lame attempt" to make the workplace fun by taking a day out of a busy workweek and assigning more work to do "stupid" things was just the last straw. Avery is crushed.

When it comes to teams, you've probably noticed that when there's trouble brewing, it can put a serious damper on innovation (see Strategy 1 on how constructive conflict contributes to change processes). We've been in the facilitation game for a while now, and while we love getting teams engaged and involved, we've come to realize that being a good facilitator isn't enough when it comes to resolving team conflicts.

We had a bit of an eye-opening moment when we were brought in to help after some team coaching sessions conducted by other facilitators. Despite everyone's best intentions, the team ended up being sorted into categories that they were using as excuses for behavior with one another, and the tough stuff was swept under the rug. That's when we realized that team coaching isn't the same as dealing with team conflicts where team mediation is needed. It's like comparing apples and oranges.

Don't get us wrong: we're all for team-building activities. Taking time away from the daily grind to bond and brainstorm is important. But we believe it's equally important to equip teams with conflict resolution skills right from the start. When teams can talk openly about disagreements and find common ground, they're better equipped to handle change and innovation. But here's the thing: we're not sold on those assessments that label employees and sort them into neat little boxes. Sure, some people swear by them, but we've seen too many instances where they just create more division instead of bringing people together. Plus, they can be used as excuses for bad behavior, which isn't helpful at all.

When a team is in trouble, you've got to act fast. The longer conflicts linger, the worse they get. We've seen it firsthand— people leaving because the team just can't get along. That's why we believe in taking a proactive approach. It's all about setting teams up for success from the get-go—clear roles, regular check-ins with leadership and customers, and a diverse mix of perspectives. And before you dive into any team sessions, take a step back and ask yourself: What's the real problem we're trying to solve here? It's like diagnosing a medical issue—you've got to understand what's going on before you can attempt to fix it. We're all about having those real conversations with leaders to get to the root cause of the issue.

Pre-Team Mediation Prep Work

As a first step, accurate identification of both business and interpersonal issues on the team is essential. The team sessions demand significant investments of both time and money. Leaders often inadvertently introduce unnecessary complexity into their environments. They may struggle to maintain clarity about the objectives they aim to achieve and require your assistance in defining a clear path forward. Leaders might also cling to unworkable initiatives or become mired in overthinking and overengineering, losing sight of essential priorities. While leaders may turn to climate surveys or team assessments for guidance when faced with team troubles, we believe these resources are frequently overused and fail to provide meaningful insights. While we do incorporate such surveys and assessments into our engagements if available, our approach prioritizes initiating in-depth conversations with leaders. This allows us to grasp their specific concerns and understand the business implications of the conflicts at hand before proceeding further.

To be even clearer, the reason why the business impact matters is pretty straightforward. While it would be ideal to have a team where everyone gets along perfectly, the reality is that a few disagreements or personal conflicts don't necessarily warrant immediate intervention. What truly matters is whether these issues are affecting the team's performance and productivity beyond a day or two or repeatedly. In fact, constantly trying to resolve personal conflicts between team members can sometimes do more harm than good. It can create unnecessary tension and frustration among team members who feel like their time and energy are being wasted on non–work-related issues.

Recently, leadership development has been really big on boosting empathy skills, and we're totally on board with that. Empathy is super important for leaders because it helps them connect with their teams on a deeper level and make the workplace more inclusive and supportive. But it's important to find a balance. While sorting out personal conflicts is key, leaders also need to keep their eyes on the big picture strategic goals. As HR partners, our job is to help leaders strike that balance. We get that empathy rocks, but leaders can't get bogged down by every little issue. Many teams can handle minor conflicts on their own, and we're here to guide leaders on when to step in and when to let the team handle things themselves. By promoting empathy while also keeping an eye on time management, leaders can create workplaces where both productivity and positivity flourish.

To that end, we want to clarify that while we advocate for a balanced approach, we're not implying that HR or leaders should shy away from addressing conflicts that cause business problems. On the contrary, addressing conflicts head-on is often necessary for growth and improvement within teams. Initiating a discussion about the potential impact of addressing conflicts typically paves the way for a productive conversation about the return on investment of intervening with the team.

HR can show their strategic partnership by leading this return on investment conversation. Measuring the cost of conflict on a team involves considering many tangible and intangible factors such as—

1. *Productivity loss.* Have team members and managers spent more time on addressing conflicts instead of focusing on team tasks. This can also be increased interruptions, decreased collaboration, and stalled projects caused by unresolved conflicts. What are the opportunity costs—which are what might have been possible with a team working smoothly?

2. *Employee turnover.* Are conflicts contributing to dissatisfaction and subsequent departures? What is the cost to recruit, hire, onboard, and train replacement employees?

3. *Absenteeism.* Has there been an uptick in sick leave usage?

4. *Quality of work.* Does the same team now make frequent mistakes, are there delays, or are the customers starting to complain? Is the leader noticing a lack of engagement ("I quit but I forgot to tell you") from previously engaged employees?

5. *Legal and compliance risks.* Has there been an uptick in formal grievances or an inattention to policy?

This conversation is greatly facilitated by thorough preparation and a curious mindset from the HR professional both prior to and during conversations with leaders. HR professionals will delve deeply into understanding various aspects of the team dynamics, including roles, the number of employees in the organization, its mission, staffing turnover rates, and any ongoing challenges faced by the company or organization. This comprehensive understanding ensures that HR approaches interventions with a well-rounded perspective informed by data and insights into the specific context of the team and organization.

To get to the heart of the conflict itself, consider asking the following:

1. *Leadership tenure.* How long have you been leading this team, and have there been any recent changes in leadership positions?

2. *Conflict awareness.* How did you become aware of the conflict within the team?

3. *Root causes.* What do you believe are the primary reasons behind the conflict?

4. *Impact assessment.* What impact is the relationship problem having on the team's productivity and output?

> **HR TIP:** Distinguish between interpersonal and task-related issues and record them separately.

5. *Team state.* Would you describe the team's current state as typical, or are there external factors contributing to increased stress or workload?

6. *Goals for intervention.* What are the top two objectives you hope to achieve through this team mediation process?

> **HR TIP:** If a few individuals are central to the conflict, first focus mediation efforts on them rather than involving the entire team, who may become frustrated.

7. *Identifying influencers.* Are there specific individuals who appear to be influencing the conflict dynamics, and are there others who seem to remain silent?

8. *Session attendance.* How many team members will be participating in the session?

9. *External impact.* What effects might the conflict have on sister organizations, external stakeholders, or internal business partnerships?

HR TIP: Keep the group as small as possible; but armed with the organization data, ask about any differences between what you expected and those participating.

10. *Conflict class versus mediation.* If the leader requested a conflict resolution training session rather than a facilitated session, why?

11. *Logistical details.* Tell the leader your version of the following: "I anticipate requiring one more meeting with you in approximately a week's time. I'll also need your assistance in announcing my engagement to the team. The session itself will span a full day, with some pre- and post-work. Could you suggest an ideal date and time that aligns with your team's schedules? Are there any particular time frames I should avoid?"

HR TIP: If the leader suggests less than a full day is needed, it may be your indication that a facilitated team-building activity would suffice.

Send your questions in advance, along with a brief biography of yourself and your cofacilitator, as we typically recommend you conduct team engagements with two facilitators for optimal effectiveness.

The Team Mediation Process

Do you realize what sets HR professionals apart as facilitators, even if you may need to collaborate with someone more experienced in handling large group dynamics? You bring a unique perspective as an insider business partner, plus you now possess insights gained from reading this book. Embarking on a team mediation endeavor for the first time can feel daunting, so it's important to remember that mastery of any new skill comes with practice, and imperfection is part of the learning process. The important point to grasp is that only you will be aware of any initial hesitations or uncertainties on your part.

Engage in thorough preparation and stand alongside the employees during this challenging period with empathy and understanding for the pressures they may be under. The leadership aspect of this role is something you inherently embody, but the bulk of the effort lies in empowering the leader and team to navigate the conflict resolution process themselves. While it's possible to delegate this leadership role, consider the potential risks to your reputation. If you do decide to outsource this work, this chapter aims to equip you with the tools to pose insightful questions before entrusting someone else with the task, ensuring that they contribute positively to the organization's dynamics rather than exacerbate existing issues.

Now that we have gathered preliminary information, it's time to map out your approach to the mediation process. Let's take a step back and look at the big picture. The following is an outline and overview of each stage of a typical team mediation event flow. We refer to this flow as the "I, We, We, I" model, emphasizing the importance of individual reflection and group collaboration throughout the process.

We strongly encourage you to utilize this model as a framework for collaboration with your cofacilitator. By sitting down together and planning the engagement at each stage, you can ensure a cohesive and effective mediation experience for all participants. This collaborative approach will help guide the team toward resolution while fostering a sense of ownership and accountability for the outcomes achieved. Before delving into the details of each step, it's beneficial to start by outlining the overall picture and purpose of each stage:

Team Mediation Stages

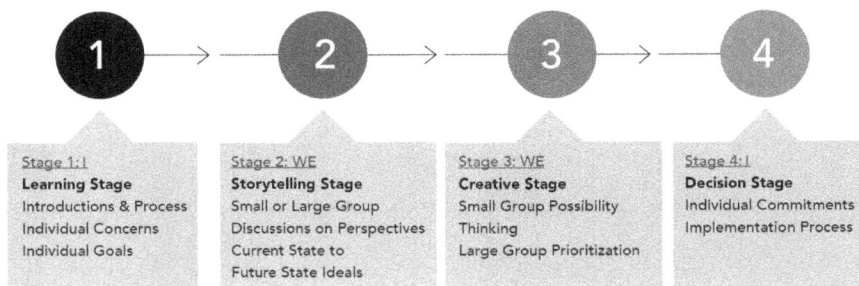

Stage 1: I	Stage 2: WE	Stage 3: WE	Stage 4: I
Learning Stage	**Storytelling Stage**	**Creative Stage**	**Decision Stage**
Introductions & Process	Small or Large Group	Small Group Possibility	Individual Commitments
Individual Concerns	Discussions on Perspectives	Thinking	Implementation Process
Individual Goals	Current State to	Large Group Prioritization	
	Future State Ideals		

STAGE 1 I—LEARNING STAGE

Introduction:

1. Begin by introducing the purpose and objectives of the mediation session.

2. Establish a safe and respectful environment for open dialogue.

3. Outline the structure and expectations for the session.

Individual concerns:

1. Provide each participant with an opportunity to express their individual concerns and perspectives.

2. Encourage active listening and empathy from all participants.

3. Use reflective listening techniques to ensure understanding and validation of each person's concerns.

Individual goals:

1. Facilitate a discussion where participants articulate their individual goals for the mediation process.

2. Encourage participants to consider both personal and collective objectives.

3. Help individuals identify areas where they hope to see improvement or resolution.

STAGE 2 WE—STORYTELLING STAGE

Large group discussions on perspectives:

1. Transition into a group discussion where participants share their perspectives on the current state of the team dynamics.

2. Encourage storytelling and narrative sharing to deepen understanding of each other's experiences.

3. Facilitate active listening and respectful dialogue to ensure all voices are heard.

Current state to future state ideals:

1. Guide the group in envisioning an ideal future state for the team.

2. Encourage participants to reflect on what success looks like for them personally and as a team.

3. Facilitate discussions on the values, behaviors, and practices that align with the desired future state.

Gap analysis:

1. Lead the group in a gap analysis exercise to identify discrepancies between the current state and the desired future state.

2. Encourage participants to explore root causes of existing challenges and barriers to progress.

3. Facilitate discussions on potential strategies for bridging the identified gaps.

STAGE 3 WE—CREATIVE STAGE

Small group possibility brainstorming:

1. Divide participants into smaller groups to engage in brainstorming sessions.

2. Encourage creativity and innovation in exploring potential solutions to address the identified gaps.

3. Provide support and guidance as needed to facilitate productive brainstorming sessions.

Gap analysis between Stage 2 and Stage 3:

1. Reconvene the larger group to discuss the outcomes of the small group brainstorming sessions.

2. Facilitate a collective reflection on the ideas generated and their potential impact on bridging the identified gaps.

3. Encourage participants to identify common themes and prioritize actionable steps for moving forward.

STAGE 4 I—DECISION STAGE

Large group decision analysis:

1. Lead the group in a structured decision-making process to evaluate the proposed solutions and determine the most viable course of action.

2. Encourage critical thinking and consensus-building among participants.

3. Facilitate discussions on potential risks and benefits associated with each option.

Individual commitments:

1. Ask each participant to make a commitment to specific actions or behaviors that contribute to the agreed-upon solutions.

2. Encourage accountability and follow-through by setting clear expectations for individual contributions.

Implementation process:

1. Outline the steps for implementing the decisions made during the mediation session.

2. Assign responsibilities and establish timelines for completing action items.

3. Encourage ongoing communication and collaboration to ensure the successful implementation of agreed-upon solutions.

As an HR professional, your deep understanding of your organization positions you to make informed decisions about how best to engage your teams. Recognizing that each team possesses its own unique personality, and that every HR facilitator brings their own style and preferences to the table, customization is key. Consider the team's composition and dynamics when tailoring your approach. Is the team more inclined toward analytical thinking? If so, allocating more time to small group work may resonate better. Or, if the team hails from the training department, they might thrive in large group engagements using dynamic brainstorming techniques.

Investing time in courses related to brainstorming or team dynamics can complement your conflict resolution expertise, enriching your toolkit with valuable resources. If you find yourself in a time crunch, tapping into your organization's internal strategic project planning experts, such as those versed in Agile or Lean Six Sigma methodologies, can provide valuable insights and support.

Insider HR Pro Mediating Team Tips

It's not uncommon for HR professionals to hesitate when it comes to facilitating large group mediations. One reason for this hesitation could be their previous experience with team-building exercises, leading them to overcomplicate the team mediation process or feel like they need to do fun or engaging activities. In team mediation events, this can be counterproductive or construed as dismissing the seriousness of the situation. Conflict mediation is not a team build. There are problems; it's costing the organization money, and there are employees in the room who are frustrated, emotional, or doubtful about the value of the day. In addition, it's important to recognize that mediation in a team setting differs significantly from one-on-one interventions. While mediators in two-person scenarios are directly involved in the discussions, team mediations largely rely on the team members themselves to drive the conversation forward, with the mediator primarily focusing on creating the right environment and facilitating the process. There's a humorous anecdote among employees about HR's penchant for organizing quirky and time-consuming team events, so take the pressure off yourself to be entertaining.

We recommend utilizing AI to assist in creating agendas for group facilitation sessions. By leveraging AI tools, facilitators can streamline the agenda creation process, optimize time allocation, and incorporate data-driven insights to enhance meeting outcomes. One effective way to do this is by using AI-powered scheduling assistants or agenda generation platforms, which can analyze participant preferences, past meeting outcomes, and relevant data to generate tailored agendas. This approach not only saves time but also ensures that agendas are well-structured and aligned with the objectives of the session, ultimately leading to more productive and successful group facilitation experiences.

With simplicity as our guiding principle, let's explore some HR pro tips tailored to each stage of the mediation process:

STAGE 1 I—LEARNING STAGE TIPS

The title of this stage is appropriate. This is where we learn about the process, how the leader feels about the team conflict, and how each employee will contribute to the solution. We need to set up a team mediation with clear expectations and with employees contributing thoughts right away.

1. *Leader's role.* The organizational leader should kick off the session with brief remarks outlining the purpose and top goals. It's essential that leaders actively participate in these engagements, as they are integral members of the team. Avoid creating artificial situations by excluding leaders, as their presence fosters transparency and accountability. Small group work is essential, with

leaders rotating among different groups to ensure their involvement and perspective.

Sample Opening Speech for Team Leaders

Good [morning/afternoon/evening] team, I want to thank you for being here today for this important team event. I appreciate your willingness to participate as we work together to address any challenges and strengthen our team dynamics.

Conflict is a natural part of any workplace, and it's essential that we address it openly and constructively. Today's event is an opportunity for us to come together, communicate honestly, and find resolutions that benefit us all. Our goal here is not to assign blame or dwell on past grievances, but rather to listen to each other, seek common ground, and commit to move forward as a more united team. Each of you brings valuable perspectives and insights to the table, and I personally cannot wait to hear them.

From my perspective, here's the business problem we are here to resolve [place a brief statement here]. However, that's only my perspective and I'm open to hearing other perspectives and ideas. I'm going to turn this over to [facilitator names] to help us with our process today. Let's get started.

2. *Facilitator introduction.* Each facilitator should introduce themselves, along with any supporting scribes, if available.

3. *Discussion of process.* Briefly introduce the agenda you created using the I, We, We, I process flow.

4. *Flow explanation.* Provide a clear overview of the session flow as outlined in the model.

5. *Note-taking protocol.* Discuss how notes will be captured, emphasizing the importance of accurately reflecting each contributor's input.

6. *Inclusive environment.* Foster a culture where all ideas are welcomed and valued. Instead of a traditional "parking lot" imagery, consider creative alternatives like a "refrigerator" to keep ideas fresh for future discussion and a "pool" where ideas can briefly and happily hang out before being revisited.

7. *Active engagement.* Begin the session by involving everyone right from the start. One way to do this is by starting with an interactive activity. For instance, you could ask each employee to share their favorite conflict quote and briefly explain why it's meaningful to them. In larger

groups, encourage mingling and sharing between participants, allowing them to connect with as many colleagues as possible within the allotted time. Another engaging option is to use picture cards depicting various art photos, which can be purchased. You can ask employees to choose cards that represent how they envision conflict resolution within the team. This hands-on approach helps to set a dynamic tone for the session and encourages participation from all team members. If the session is virtual, utilize breakout rooms and dynamically move employees around them so they meet many employees.

8. *Team behavior norms.* Bring the group back together to focus on establishing team behavior norms. If possible, arrange teams in a circle to promote eye contact, although virtual arrangements can also be effective. Encourage the team to co-create and display these agreed-upon norms prominently throughout the session to serve as a visual reminder. Guide the discussion by gently asking questions such as, "Which of these behavior rules may not be applicable or effective in our team's context?" and "Can we commit to incorporating these norms into our future interactions?" Typically, teams address concepts such as respect, courtesy, active listening, avoiding interruptions, and honest communication. Prompt deeper reflection on topics like flexibility and accountability. Encourage team members to consider

how these principles can enhance collaboration and contribute to a more positive team dynamic. By collectively establishing and committing to these behavior norms, teams can foster a culture of mutual respect, effective communication, and accountability that extends beyond the duration of the session.

9. *Team conflict behavior norms.* Following the initial engagement activity involving sharing conflict quotes or using picture cards, the facilitator guides a brief discussion to explore the insights gained regarding desired team conflict behaviors. The facilitator prompts participants to reflect on the shared quotes or selected images and identify the behaviors that resonate most positively with the team's objectives. These identified desired behaviors are then compiled into a separate list, serving as a foundation for establishing clear conflict behavior norms within the team. The facilitator encourages open dialogue by asking participants to consider what types of behaviors could potentially hinder productive conflict resolution within the team context. Participants are invited to share their perspectives on behaviors that may impede constructive conflict resolution and discuss how these behaviors could be addressed or mitigated. By openly acknowledging potential challenges and collaboratively identifying strategies for addressing them, the team can proactively establish norms that

promote healthy conflict resolution and constructive communication. This process fosters a shared understanding of the team's approach to managing conflict and reinforces a commitment to fostering a positive and collaborative team environment.

10. *Transition to Stage 2.* As you wrap up the learning stage, add a personal touch. Ask each leader to share their favorite conflict quote and explain why it's meaningful to them. They'll also talk about how they plan to lead a team that lives by this wisdom. It's a chance to connect on a deeper level and set the tone for how the team can handle conflicts together.

STAGE 2 WE—STORYTELLING STAGE TIPS

In this stage, the primary objective is to ensure that every individual voice is heard loud and clear. The aim is to document both the strengths and weaknesses in team behaviors, paving the way for a comprehensive understanding of their current dynamics. In Stage 1 we established their ideals for conflict behavior; Stage 2 calls for an exploration of what's truly happening on this team to pinpoint the underlying causes of the business problem.

Eliciting input from every member of a group can be more challenging than in a three-party mediation scenario. Although there are numerous brainstorming techniques available, we particularly favor the simplicity and effectiveness of mind mapping. To facilitate this small group exercise, display the problem statement on one or more whiteboards, ensuring that each group consists of no more than five individuals. From there, you can branch out into related ideas, solutions, and challenges contributing to the identified problem statement.

To ensure active participation, distribute individual sticky notes to each employee, encouraging them to jot down their thoughts and ideas for each branch of the mind map. These notes will then be placed on the map, fostering collaboration and sparking discussion within the small groups for a duration of 20 minutes. Throughout this process, participants will be encouraged to add additional stickies as needed, enriching the mind map with diverse insights.

Once the small group discussions have concluded, reconvene as a large group to review and discuss each mind map. Examine the perspectives presented, noting both similarities and differences without immediately attempting to solve the business problem. This phase is dedicated to acknowledging and respecting the voices contributing to our collective understanding.

Finally, invite the team leader to close this stage by expressing gratitude to the team for their valuable contributions and diverse perspectives offered on the identified problem statement. This acknowledgment underscores the importance of each individual's input in the collaborative problem-solving process.

STAGE 3 WE—CREATIVE STAGE TIPS

Having identified the contributing factors to the business problem, we now enter a crucial stage where we aim to generate a plethora of ideas to address it effectively. To facilitate this creative process, we employ nominal group techniques. Here's how it works: initially, you invite all employees to independently brainstorm and write down their ideas or potential solutions. These ideas are then collected and displayed anonymously, fostering an environment where even the more introverted team members feel empowered to contribute without the influence of group dynamics.

Once all ideas are presented, the group engages in a collaborative voting process to identify the most promising solutions. Each participant is encouraged to vote by placing a star on three ideas they believe hold the most potential for addressing the business problem. It's important to note that individuals have the flexibility to vote for their own ideas or prioritize others' suggestions over their own, promoting a collective and inclusive approach to problem-solving. If meeting virtually, use breakout rooms, whiteboards, and polling functions to allow participants to vote.

To wrap up this stage, the leader gives a big thanks to everyone for being so creative and involved in the brainstorming session. This not only shows how much each person's ideas matter, but also encourages continued collaboration as we move forward in finding effective solutions to the identified business challenge.

STAGE 4 I—DECISION STAGE TIPS

In today's fast-moving environment, decisions might not be truly final because situations can change, new information can emerge, or unexpected obstacles can arise. Decisions are also often influenced by various factors such as emotions, biases, and external pressures, which can sometimes lead to reconsideration or revision. Decisions in complex or dynamic environments may require ongoing evaluation and adjustment to ensure their effectiveness over time. In essence, the fluidity of decision-making reflects the ever-evolving nature of circumstances and the need for adaptability in response to changing conditions. So for team mediation, this decision stage is how the team will hold themselves accountable moving forward. Having the leader actively involved in this stage allows for realistic timelines and commitments.

In contrast to three-party mediations, where capturing and assigning ideas can be relatively straightforward, we've discovered that efficiently managing the time of a team to capture and assign prioritized ideas poses a significant challenge. During the decision stage, the mediator addresses the concept of decision-making, distinguishing what constitutes a decision and what doesn't.

To streamline the process, the mediator commits to providing a shared platform or document where all pertinent information, including prioritized ideas, will be documented for follow-up action planning. This ensures that all ideas are properly accounted for and accessible to team members for future reference.

The power of AI can be harnessed for group facilitation. AI algorithms have the remarkable capability to sift through vast amounts of data accumulated during meetings and group discussions, discerning key themes, sentiments, and patterns from the dialogue. This analytical prowess furnishes invaluable insights that can profoundly inform decision-making processes within the group. By extrapolating from the data, AI can offer groups data-driven recommendations, conduct simulations, and perform scenario analyses to meticulously evaluate various options and their potential outcomes. Through AI's computational prowess, groups gain access to a comprehensive understanding of the implications of their choices, enabling them to make informed decisions that align with their objectives and mitigate risks effectively.

The mediator leads a discussion centered on the commitment to take ownership of the ideas collectively identified as the team's voice. This encourages each team member to not only contribute ideas but also to actively participate in implementing and driving forward the agreed-upon solutions. By fostering a sense of ownership and accountability among team members, the decision-making process becomes more collaborative and impactful.

Sample Final Closing Thoughts for Team Leaders

Team, as we bring our team mediation to a close, I want to give a big shout-out to everyone here. Today we tackled some tough stuff, had some real talks, and I've got to say that I'm blown away by the honesty and teamwork I've seen. It takes guts to be real, and I appreciate each and every one of you for bringing your honesty and openness to the table.

I'm especially encouraged by the team behavioral norms we adopted today. I want us to hold one another accountable to them. Let's keep the momentum going. Let's keep talking, keep supporting each other, and just know that great can still get greater. I'm excited to see where we go from here. Thanks for being awesome, everyone!

Managing Difficult Group Conversations

Facilitating difficult conversations in a large group setting isn't easy, but it's really the point of the entire event! Here are some strategies:

1. *Refer back to the objectives and ground rules.* Before diving into the conversation, ensure everyone understands the purpose and goals. Set ground rules for communication,

emphasizing respect, active listening, and avoiding personal attacks. Clear guidelines provide structure and keep the discussion focused on the business problem solutions.

2. *Promote active listening and participation.* Encourage participants to actively listen to one another without interruption.

3. *Validate emotions and guide constructive dialogue.* Emotions can escalate during difficult conversations, making it important to acknowledge and validate participants' feelings. Redirect the conversation back to constructive dialogue if it veers off track, utilizing techniques like reframing to shift focus toward finding solutions.

4. *Exhibit calmness and confidence.* As the mediator, your demeanor sets the tone for the discussion. Maintain a calm and composed presence, even if you feel uncertain or challenged. Projecting confidence in your role as an HR leader reassures participants and encourages open communication.

5. *Examine your personal responses to conflict.* Prior to leading a team mediation, reflect on your own responses to conflict and develop strategies for managing them effectively. Understand your triggers and biases, and practice techniques for remaining neutral and impartial during challenging conversations. After each conflict conversation you engage in—whether that is coaching,

third-party resolution, or team mediation events—take the time to learn from these valuable learning opportunities by reflecting on what you did well and what you'd do differently next time.

Managing Confidentiality

Ensuring confidentiality serves as a cornerstone in fostering trust and cultivating a safe environment for all participants within a team event. While acknowledging the inevitable discourse surrounding such gatherings, it's important to implement measures that uphold confidentiality while still allowing for fruitful discussions. Here are several proactive steps to navigate this delicate balance:

1. *Ground rules.* Let participants know that what is discussed during the event should remain within the confines of the team and should not be shared outside of it.

2. *Define confidentiality.* Make sure participants understand what confidentiality means in the context of the event. Explain that it includes not disclosing personal stories, opinions shared, or any sensitive information discussed during the event.

3. *Assure mediator confidentiality.* Reassure participants that you, as the mediator, will also maintain confidentiality.

This can help build trust and encourage participants to open up during discussions.

4. *Gain agreement.* Educate participants on the significance of confidentiality and its role in fostering a supportive and inclusive environment. Raise awareness about the potential consequences of breaching confidentiality and emphasize the value of trust in building cohesive teams. If you decide to implement formal confidentiality agreements, we encourage you to seek your counsel's advice and perhaps call them "pledges" instead of "signed agreements." A team will have shared outputs and the goal is for them to be discussed when implemented. Our personal experience has shown the pitfalls outweigh the benefits of signed confidentiality agreements for team mediation events.

Measuring Success

Assessing the effectiveness of team mediation events—despite their demanding time commitments—is essential, especially for those of us who prefer practical outcomes over extensive surveying and data analysis. Acknowledging that some organizational contexts mandate accountability, self-reflection on our mediation efforts can inform future improvements. Our fundamental belief is that all mediations yield success, as they equip teams with greater insights post-event and establish behavioral norms facilitating constructive dialogue among leaders and teammates. To gauge the impact of our team mediation, we propose the following criteria:

1. *Assess goals.* Did you meet your goals? Think about what you set out to achieve and see if you actually did. Did you get everyone to open up a bit more? We placed "I" in our model for a reason: "I" means the individual employee's voice. In team conflicts, individual voices can get lost, and it is your job to respect and open up space for individual needs.

2. *Gather feedback.* Get feedback from managers immediately after the mediation event and follow up several months later to gauge any sustained improvements. This feedback loop provides valuable insights into the perceived effectiveness of the mediation and its impact on team dynamics. Don't forget that AI tools can collect feedback from participants anonymously and analyze it to identify areas for improvement in group dynamics, meeting effectiveness, or facilitation techniques.

3. *Revisit notes.* Review your notes taken during previous discussions about the cost of conflict within the organization. Use these insights to inform discussions with participants about any observed improvements in communication, collaboration, or conflict resolution skills following the mediation event.

4. *Evaluate the long-term impact.* After the mediation event, assess long-term organizational metrics such as turnover rates, sick leave, formal grievances, and overall employee satisfaction. Look for trends indicating a reduction in negative outcomes associated with unresolved conflicts or ineffective communication.

5. *Keep a record.* Maintain a running record of case studies and success stories highlighting the positive outcomes of mediation events. Sharing these with future managers can illustrate value.

By utilizing these evaluation methods, organizations can effectively measure the success of team mediation events and demonstrate their value in promoting healthier workplace dynamics, fostering collaboration, and reducing the negative impacts of unresolved conflicts.

As we bring this chapter on team mediation to a close, we want to leave you with a sense of empowerment and inspiration. In this chapter's opening anecdote, we witnessed the HR expert handing over the responsibility of facilitating Avery's team mediation to someone else. This decision had three important consequences. First, HR missed the opportunity to be recognized as the strategic business partner for Avery from start to finish. Second, the HR expert could have provided Avery with valuable insights and guidance to ensure the offsite was tailored to the organization's specific needs, and adjust quickly as the day proceeded. Third,

HR lost the chance to gain a deep understanding of Avery's issues and challenges. Firsthand involvement in such events allows HR professionals to gather valuable insights into the organization's culture, dynamics, and areas for future improvement.

Our aim throughout this journey has been to provide you with a framework—an adaptable roadmap that you can tailor to fit the unique contours of your organization's landscape. We hope that the team mediation process we've outlined here has sparked your imagination and encouraged you to envision modifications that align seamlessly with your organization's culture, values, and objectives.

As you reflect on the process we've explored together, we invite you to notice the simplicity inherent in each step. By keeping things clear, concise, and focused, we've created space for deliberate, meaningful engagement with both the team behavior norms and the underlying business problem. This simplicity is intentional—it's a deliberate choice to strip away the extraneous and focus on what truly matters.

Critical Thinking Questions

1. After reading this process, what steps do you foresee as most challenging? How will you work with your cofacilitator to acknowledge these and seek support?

2. How will you handle potentially difficult or emotional conversations that may arise?

3. How will you evaluate the success of the mediation process? What outcomes are you hoping to achieve?

4. In what ways can you dedicate yourself to integrating AI into your sessions, and what guidance does AI offer regarding facilitation strategies that you already align with?

Culture Perspectives: Fostering Diversity of Ideas

Jamie, a representative of her company's newcomer's cohort, visits Tom from the Recruitment Department of HR to discuss a generation gap issue within the organization. Jamie expresses frustration at her ideas being overlooked by senior employees. Feeling like a misfit, Jamie has considered leaving for another company. Upon sharing her concerns with friends, she discovers that peers from the same cohort face similar challenges. The HR department recruits top talent from prestigious colleges but observes that their innovative ideas are being stifled. Jamie highlights her efforts to contribute new ideas in meetings, only to see them overshadowed or disregarded. Tom believes the problem isn't a generation gap, but lies more in the organization's culture of high-performing "heroes" who prefer to work alone and are not used to having their ideas challenged or debated. Tom fears he should have better prepared the workforce for this new generation of high-performing and team-orientated employees.

"Workplace culture" refers to the shared core values, attitudes, and behaviors that are present in a workplace. This culture is not defined by mere words, but is reflected in the observable behaviors of individuals as they interact with one another day to day. As it relates to conflict, preparing a fertile ground in a current workplace for new and diverse perspectives is one of the most overlooked aspects of implementing culture change. Fundamentally, for constructive debate to flourish, we embrace a workplace culture centered on meaningful interactions—a culture of encounter. A culture of encounter prioritizes diverse perspectives to the extent that it actively celebrates and embraces different viewpoints as a primary way to engage with new ideas. In this culture, upon being introduced to a new concept by team members or collaborators, a leader consistently inquires about the collaborators involved and requests that the initial discussion on the topic includes all relevant individuals present in the room.

HR is the change agent that helps establish and later supports a culture of encounter. You champion a workplace that creates a setting where shared core company or organizational values and practices define the organization both internally for employees and are visible to stakeholders externally. This culture emphasizes reaching out, fostering dialogue, and building relationships with one another to promote understanding and collaboration. When new ideas emerge, the initial focus is on recognizing their merits rather than scrutinizing their shortcomings.

Diversity, particularly in the context of conflict, revolves around embracing differences in ideas and thoughts—a value many of us claim to uphold. Despite companies and organizations globally emphasizing the importance of hiring for diverse thinking, conflicts arise when these thoughts diverge. The act of reaching out to consider others' ideas is closely linked to empathy and the ability to take different perspectives. Practicing empathy can be challenging, especially when one lacks experience with another person's viewpoint. In reality, when exposed to someone else's perspective, sympathy often emerges more prominently than empathy. We might think or say, "I'm sorry you're going through this," or, "That must be really hard." It is important to recognize that sympathy, although common, may not always align with what the other person seeks in a relationship.

Consider this: many organizations invest significant portions of their budget in conveying their commitment to respecting diverse perspectives. This often involves the establishment of dedicated teams for cultural transformation or the creation of innovation departments. But these endeavors frequently encounter hurdles. For instance, innovation departments may inadvertently disrupt existing workflows as they integrate themselves into teams, resulting in a loss of momentum. Despite these efforts, there's only one strategy we've discovered that truly impacts an organization's conflict culture: equipping all employees with the skills necessary to generate and nurture ideas effectively. We believe you should teach your organization's employees how to birth an idea. This "all hands" skill-building approach fosters a culture where diverse thoughts are valued and conflicts about which ideas are best are managed constructively, ultimately contributing to the organization's growth and success.

To that end, we believe these are three core skills every employee must develop in order to respect diverse ideas and still be seen as efficient and effective on the job. In the following sections we discuss perspective seeking, active listening, and open-mindedness.

Key Conflict Skill: Perspective Seeking

Fostering a culture of constructive debate of great ideas starts with teaching the skill traditionally known as perspective taking. When faced with conflicts or decisions, instead of the traditional notion of perspective taking, we advocate for a shift toward perspective seeking in the early stages of conflict resolution or before the mediation event and perspective sharing during the communication exchange with each other. The term "perspective taking" can inadvertently imply surrendering one's own viewpoint for another, which may feel uncomfortable or like a loss. In contrast, perspective seeking emphasizes actively exploring different viewpoints without compromising one's own beliefs. For instance, in the coat shopping analogy we mentioned earlier, if you need the coat for skiing but lack experience, your shopping partner's skiing expertise could provide crucial insights, preventing potential mistakes and revealing blind spots you might have otherwise missed.

By engaging in perspective seeking, you open yourself to diverse viewpoints in other topics, even if initially unfamiliar or challenging. Perspective seeking is a skill that can be cultivated over time by being open to reevaluating your initial perspectives and embracing the potential for personal growth and new insights. It should be a core skill taught in all conflict management classes.

Methods for teaching perspective thinking:

1. *Role-playing exercises.* Scenarios where employees can take on different roles within a given situation allow them to understand perspectives other than their own. It also helps them develop empathy toward their colleagues' viewpoints.

2. *Case studies.* Presenting real-life or hypothetical but realistic scenarios that employees may encounter in their work and encouraging them to analyze the situation from multiple perspectives helps employees expand their viewpoints.

3. *Cross-functional team projects and shadowing.* Assigning projects that require collaboration among employees from different departments or providing shadowing opportunities encourages employees to consider perspectives outside their own team or role.

4. *Team-building activities on perspective taking.* Especially when standing up new teams, playing games like "Would You Rather" provides a playful yet meaningful platform for individuals to explore different viewpoints and challenges. By engaging in these activities, employees recognize the complexities of convincing others to adopt alternative perspectives.

Key Conflict Skill: Active Listening

To hear a different perspective, employees need to improve their active listening skills. Encourage employees to listen attentively to others without interrupting. This includes giving their full attention, paraphrasing what they've heard to ensure understanding, and asking clarifying questions. We use the acronym FOCUS to provide a quick model for what we mean by active listening in conflict idea generating:

1. *F—full attention.* Silence your mind. Encourage employees to give their full attention to the speaker, avoiding multitasking or distractions.

2. *O—open-mindedness.* Stress the importance of maintaining an open mind, being receptive to the speaker's ideas and perspectives, even if they differ from their own.

3. *C—clarify.* Prompt employees to seek clarification when needed by paraphrasing and asking open-ended questions to ensure they fully understand the speaker's message.

4. *U—understand emotions.* Stress the importance of tuning into the speaker's emotions, both through verbal and nonverbal cues, and empathizing with their feelings.

5. *S—summarize.* Suggest that employees summarize the speaker's main points periodically to demonstrate understanding and ensure clarity.

Using the FOCUS acronym can help employees remember the key aspects of active listening and apply them effectively in workplace interactions, fostering better communication and understanding.

Teaching employees active listening using the FOCUS acronym:

Create visual aids such as a small hand-held posters or graphics that highlight each aspect of the FOCUS acronym along with examples. For example—

1. Employees are split into pairs for this exercise. In each pair, one person shares a personal workplace conflict experience where they felt particularly affected, perhaps due to feeling unappreciated or micromanaged. This individual acts as the storyteller.

2. The other person in the pair takes on the role of the active listener. They practice applying the FOCUS method for a duration of 15 minutes while attentively listening to the storyteller's account.

3. Following the listening exercise, the pair engages in a discussion where they reflect on their experiences. They share insights on how it felt both to actively listen and to be listened to uninterrupted for the entire 15-minute duration. This discussion allows participants to explore the dynamics of effective listening and communication in a real-life context, fostering greater understanding and empathy among employees.

Key Conflict Skill: Open-Mindedness

Teach employees to approach conflicts with an open mind, being willing to consider alternative viewpoints and solutions. Different than perspective-seeking training, we must teach employees to challenge their own assumptions in order to even consider other perspectives. Bias can significantly impact conflict resolution processes, potentially leading to unfair outcomes or exacerbating existing tensions. These biases can especially show up during debate of ideas. Some common biases that we've seen show up when debating new ideas are—

- *Confirmation bias.* This bias occurs when individuals seek out or interpret information in a way that confirms their existing beliefs or hypotheses. In conflict resolution, this can lead to the dismissal of evidence that contradicts one's viewpoint or the favoring of information that supports one party over another.

    Let's say a team is discussing potential strategies for improving productivity. Two team members, Alex and Tracy, propose different approaches. Alex suggests implementing a new software tool, while Tracy suggests restructuring the team's workflow. During the discussion, Alex strongly advocates for the software tool, presenting research studies and testimonials from other companies that have successfully used similar tools to boost productivity. Meanwhile, Tracy argues for the workflow restructuring, providing examples of how it has worked in the past for other teams and citing expert opinions on the benefits of such changes.

    Now, imagine that the team leader, Chris, has a personal preference for technological solutions and has previously implemented software tools in other projects with success. Chris listens attentively to Alex's arguments, nodding in agreement and asking clarifying questions. But when Tracy presents her case for workflow restructuring, Chris seems less engaged, raising doubts about its effectiveness and expressing concerns about disrupting the current workflow. In this scenario, Chris is exhibiting confirmation bias by favoring the solution (the software tool) that aligns with his pre-existing beliefs and experiences. Despite both proposals having merits and potential benefits, Chris's bias toward technology and previous successes leads him to disproportionately weigh the evidence presented by Alex while downplaying or dismissing Tracy's arguments.

- *Anchoring bias.* This bias involves relying too heavily on the first piece of information encountered (the "anchor") when making decisions. In conflict resolution, anchoring bias may manifest when individuals fixate on initial offers, positions, or perceptions of the situation, making it difficult to consider alternative perspectives or solutions.

  Imagine a team is discussing the budget for an upcoming project. One member suggests a budget of $100,000 based on their initial assessment of the project's requirements. Others in the team, without doing their own independent analysis, may then anchor their subsequent suggestions and arguments around this initial figure of $100,000. Even if someone later realizes that the project could be completed for much less or much more than $100,000 based on further research or market analysis, they might still unconsciously adjust their suggestions around this initial anchor. Those arguing for higher budgets might use $100,000 as the starting point and suggest additional funds from there, while those advocating for lower budgets might try to adjust downward from the anchor.

- *In-group bias.* This bias involves favoring individuals who belong to the same group as oneself. In conflict resolution, in-group bias can lead to unfair treatment of outsiders or favoritism toward one's own group members, undermining the impartiality and effectiveness of the resolution process.

Let's say there's a team at work discussing the implementation of a new project management software. Within this team, there are two distinct groups: the proponents of adopting the new software (the "innovators") and those who are skeptical or resistant to change (the "traditionalists"). In this scenario, an example of in-group bias could manifest when each group evaluates the merits and drawbacks of the new software. The innovators may tend to emphasize the potential benefits such as increased efficiency, better task tracking, and improved collaboration. They may overlook potential challenges or downsides and may be more inclined to dismiss criticisms or concerns raised by the traditionalists.

Traditionalists may be more focused on the potential

risks and disruptions associated with implementing new software. They might highlight concerns about the learning curve, compatibility issues with existing systems, or potential resistance from team members. They may downplay the potential benefits or advantages presented by the innovators. In this situation, each group is demonstrating in-group bias by favoring their own perspective and minimizing the validity of the opposing viewpoint. This bias can hinder productive discussion and decision-making, as it prevents the team from fully considering all aspects of the issue at hand.

- *Self-serving bias.* Self-serving bias involves attributing positive outcomes to one's own actions or abilities while blaming negative outcomes on external factors. In conflict resolution, this bias can hinder accountability and collaboration as parties may resist acknowledging their own contributions. Recognizing and addressing these biases is essential for impartial and effective conflict resolution processes. Techniques such as active listening, empathy-building, and encouraging perspective-taking can help mitigate the impact of biases and promote fair and constructive resolutions.

Imagine a team at work discussing the outcome of a project that didn't meet its goals. During the debate, one team member, Jennifer, consistently attributes the failure to external factors beyond her control, such as unexpected market changes or lack of support from other departments. She emphasizes her own hard work and dedication to the project.

When discussing successes or positive outcomes, Jennifer tends to attribute them primarily to her own efforts and skills, downplaying the contributions of others or external factors. This is a manifestation of the self-serving bias, where individuals tend to attribute positive outcomes to internal factors (like their abilities or efforts) while attributing negative outcomes to external factors (like luck or circumstances). In this scenario, Jennifer's tendency to attribute failures to external factors while taking full credit for successes could hinder constructive problem-solving within the team. It may lead to a lack of accountability and prevent the team from addressing underlying issues effectively.

- *Status quo bias.* One of the most common workplace biases that can cause conflict when debating new ideas is the "status quo bias." This bias refers to a tendency to prefer things to remain the same or stick to the current state of affairs, even in the face of potentially beneficial changes or innovations. When debating new ideas, individuals influenced by status quo bias may resist change, dismiss novel proposals prematurely, or cling to familiar practices out of comfort or fear of uncertainty.

Imagine a marketing team at a software company has been using traditional advertising methods such as print ads and television commercials for years. Despite the emergence of digital marketing strategies like social media advertising and influencer partnerships, the team members are resistant to change because they are comfortable with the familiar methods and believe they have been successful in the past.

When a new employee proposes reallocating a portion of the marketing budget toward digital channels, suggesting that it could potentially reach a larger and more targeted audience at a lower cost, some team members dismiss the idea outright. They argue that the company has always relied on traditional advertising and that it has worked well in the past, so there's no need to change tactics now.

In this scenario, the status quo bias is evident in the team's reluctance to consider new ideas and adapt to changing trends in the industry. Despite the potential benefits of exploring digital marketing strategies, the team's attachment to the current methods prevents them from fully evaluating and embracing innovative approaches.

Teaching about bias in the workplace, especially during the idea generation phase, is essential for fostering a culture of idea inclusivity. Here's a step-by-step approach:

1. *Introduction to bias.* Start by introducing the concept of bias and its relevance in the workplace. Explain that bias refers to unconscious tendencies or preferences that

can influence decision-making and perception. Provide examples of common biases such as confirmation bias, anchoring bias, and the self-serving bias. Facilitate a discussion on how they can impact idea generation and allow employees to provide examples they've seen.

2. *Role-playing scenario.* Create role-playing scenarios where participants can experience firsthand how bias can impact interactions and decision-making. Encourage them to reflect on how their own biases might influence their behavior in similar situations. Here's a simple role-play example where you would give the scenario and then let the parties do the rest with you as facilitator of the dialogue. You will note that this "facilitator" begins to cross over to the "mediator" hat.

Role-Play Scenario: The Idea Pitch

Participants: Sarah (team lead), Frank (team member), and facilitator (HR)

Scenario: Sarah, the team lead, has called a meeting to discuss potential ideas for an upcoming project. Frank, a team member, has been eager to share his ideas but has noticed that Sarah tends to favor ideas that align with her own perspective. You (HR) suspect that bias may be influ-

continued

encing the decision-making process and wants to address it constructively. You volunteer to help.

FACILITATOR: Okay, Sarah and Frank, thank you for joining me. You have asked me to help you brainstorm ideas for your new project. Sarah, as the team lead, could you kick things off by sharing your vision for this project?

SARAH: Of course. I think our main focus should be on increasing customer engagement through social media platforms. We've seen success with this approach in the past, so I believe it's the best direction for us to take.

FACILITATOR: Thank you, Sarah. Now, Frank, what are your thoughts on Sarah's idea? Do you have any alternative suggestions?

FRANK: Actually, I've been thinking about a different approach. Instead of solely focusing on social media, we could explore incorporating interactive webinars or virtual events to engage our audience more directly. I believe this could help us reach a wider demographic and create a more personalized experience for our customers.

FACILITATOR: That sounds like a promising idea, Frank. Sarah, what do you think about Frank's suggestion?

SARAH: Well, while I appreciate Frank's input, I'm not sure if virtual events align with our project goals. Social media has been a proven strategy for us in the past, and I'm hesitant to deviate from that.

FACILITATOR: Frank, it seems like Sarah has some reservations about your idea. How do you feel about that?

FRANK: I understand Sarah's perspective, but I believe it's important for us to explore different options before making a decision. Virtual events could offer unique opportunities for engagement that we haven't considered yet.

FACILITATOR: Sarah, do you think there might be any bias influencing our decision-making process here?

SARAH: Well, now that you mention it, I can see how my preference for social media might be influencing my judgment. I'll admit I haven't given Frank's idea enough consideration.

FACILITATOR: Thank you for your honesty, Sarah. This is a perfect example of how bias can subtly influence our decision-making process. By acknowledging and addressing our biases, we can ensure that all ideas are given fair consideration. Let's take some time to explore both options further and reconvene to make a more informed decision.

In this role-playing scenario, the facilitator effectively raises concerns about bias influencing the decision-making process, prompting Sarah to reflect on her own perspective and biases. Through open dialogue and constructive feedback, the team can work toward a more inclusive and effective decision-making process.

1. *Tools and techniques for mitigating bias.* Introduce practical tools and techniques for mitigating bias during idea generation. This could include using structured decision-making frameworks like pros and cons analysis, Strengths, Weaknesses, Opportunities, and Threats (SWOT) analysis, decision trees, and cost-benefit analysis.

2. *Feedback and reflection.* Encourage participants to reflect on their own biases and how they might impact their contributions to idea generation. Provide opportunities for open dialogue and feedback to foster a culture of continuous learning and improvement.

The Right Environment

Creating a culture that values new ideas requires intentional effort and a combination of strategies to foster an environment where creativity and innovation can thrive. Here are some steps you can take to set up such a culture:

1. *Leadership commitment.* Leadership plays an important role in setting the tone for the organization. Leaders

should openly express their support for new ideas and innovation, and they should lead by example by embracing change themselves.

2. *Clear communication.* Clearly communicate the importance of innovation and the value placed on new ideas throughout the organization. This can be done through internal messaging, meetings, and other communication channels.

3. *Encourage risk-taking.* Create an environment where employees feel comfortable taking risks and trying out new ideas without fear of failure. Sometimes what looks like people being conflict-averse is actually them being risk-averse. Encourage experimentation and recognize that failure is often a necessary step on the path to innovation.

4. *Reward innovation.* Recognize and reward employees who contribute new ideas or who take innovative approaches to solving problems. This could include monetary rewards, promotions, or simply public recognition.

5. *Create space for creativity.* Provide physical and virtual spaces where employees can brainstorm, collaborate, and work on new ideas without interruption. This might include dedicated innovation labs, brainstorming sessions, or online platforms for idea sharing.

By implementing these strategies and fostering a culture that values new ideas, organizations can unleash the creativity of their employees. Conflict then can be seen as less of a negative aspect with a team and more of a catalyst for innovation. Here's how:

- *Divergent perspectives.* Conflict arises when there are differing perspectives or ideas within a group. This diversity of thought can lead to more comprehensive discussions and a wider range of potential solutions to a problem. By challenging each other's viewpoints, team members can uncover blind spots and consider alternative approaches, ultimately leading to more innovative solutions.

- *Critical evaluation.* Conflict encourages individuals to critically evaluate their own ideas and those of others. When faced with opposition, individuals are often compelled to defend and refine their ideas, leading to a deeper understanding of the problem and potential solutions. This process of scrutiny can help weed out weaker ideas and strengthen the ones with the most potential for innovation.

- *Creativity and innovation.* Conflict can spark creativity by forcing individuals to think outside the box and consider unconventional solutions. When faced with disagreement or opposition, people are motivated to explore new possibilities and approaches, leading to innovative breakthroughs that might not have been considered otherwise.

- *Stimulating change and adaptation.* Conflict often arises when there is a need for change or adaptation within an organization. By confronting and addressing these conflicts head-on, organizations can identify areas for improvement and innovation. Embracing conflict as a driver of change can lead to the implementation of new processes, technologies, or strategies that enhance efficiency and competitiveness.

- *Fostering collaboration and trust.* When managed constructively, conflict can strengthen relationships and foster a culture of collaboration and trust. By engaging in open and honest dialogue, team members can gain a deeper understanding of each other's perspectives and develop mutual respect. This in turn creates an environment where individuals feel comfortable sharing new ideas and taking calculated risks, ultimately driving innovation.

Conflict can serve as a powerful catalyst for innovation by promoting divergent thinking, critical thinking, creativity, and collaboration. By embracing conflict and managing it effectively, organizations can leverage it as a valuable tool for driving positive change and achieving breakthrough innovations.

HR plays a pivotal role in fostering a culture of encounter within the organization, where diverse perspectives are not only valued but actively celebrated. By championing meaningful interactions and embracing different viewpoints, HR acts as a change agent in establishing an environment where innovative ideas can flourish. As illustrated by this chapter's opening anecdote, Tom did a good job of recruiting for diversity of ideas and experiences, but did not prepare the existing workforce to embrace these new thoughts in the right way. As a result, Jamie and other new employees got off to a bad start—and sometimes that can be irreparable. Recognizing the importance of equipping employees with essential conflict resolution skills, HR endeavors to teach perspective seeking, active listening, and open-mindedness. By addressing biases in idea generation processes, HR facilitates the creation of a culture where all ideas are given fair consideration, regardless of their origin. Through leadership commitment, clear communication, encouragement of risk-taking, reward for innovation, and provision of space for creativity, HR sets the stage for conflict to be seen not as a hindrance, but as a catalyst for innovation. HR's role in cultivating a culture that respects diverse ideas is essential, paving the way for organizational growth and success.

Critical Thinking Questions

1. Can you identify an instance of bias within your own experiences in group discussions or decision-making processes? What were the impacts?

2. How might the cultivation of active listening skills contribute to a workplace culture that values diverse ideas and perspectives?

3. Reflect on a situation where you encountered conflict due to differing perspectives at work. How was the conflict managed, and what strategies were employed to reach a resolution? In hindsight, were there any biases present that may have influenced the outcome?

Building Allies: Human Capital Strategy for Conflict Management

Florence prided herself on being the resident expert on HR matters. With over 15 years of experience, she had seen and handled just about every employee issue imaginable. She stayed in her HR lane, getting daily work done with no need for strategic planning; she was too busy for that. One day, Florence got a wake-up call from Shannon, the chief of staff. Shannon showed her a report from Finance analyzing the high costs of employee turnover, production issues, and missed deadlines—all blamed on HR's poor conflict resolution interventions. Florence was caught off-guard, unable to articulate her approach to conflict resolution. To Shannon, it was clear that HR lacked a strategic plan and operated in a silo. Shannon told Florence that changes were needed. HR could no longer afford a reactive, insular approach to conflict resolution. Shannon went on to say that Florence's way of working was outdated and ineffective in today's landscape. Florence was embarrassed, frustrated, and literally had no idea what to do next.

Once HR has made the commitment to champion effective conflict resolution within the workplace, an important initial step involves crafting a comprehensive strategy targeting how an organization will recognize the value of constructive debate while reducing the cost of unproductive interpersonal conflicts. This strategic blueprint forms the cornerstone for nurturing a culture where conflicts are dealt with constructively and proactively. Good conflict strategies are holistic frameworks designed to systematically and preemptively address conflicts within an organization. It entails merging the intent of various people strategies, processes, and resources to manage conflicts effectively across different organizational levels and areas.

Leveraging Human Capital

A human capital strategy for conflict management is a comprehensive framework designed to address conflicts within an organization in a systematic and proactive manner. It involves the integration of various strategies, processes, and resources to effectively manage conflicts at different levels and across different areas of the organization. This specifically targeted strategy includes these components:

1. *Clear policies and procedures.* The establishment of clear policies and procedures governing conflict resolution within the organization. These policies outline expectations for behavior, define the types of conflicts covered, and specify the steps to be taken to address conflicts.

2. *Training and development.* Providing training and education to employees at all levels on conflict resolution skills, communication techniques, and strategies for managing conflicts constructively. This helps to build a culture of conflict competence and empowers employees to resolve conflicts effectively.

3. *Leadership commitment.* Ensuring that employees have access to resources and support services, such as mediation, counseling, or conflict coaching, to help them address conflicts as they arise. This may involve designating trained individuals or teams within the organization to provide assistance and support to employees in conflict situations.

4. *Early intervention.* Implementing mechanisms for early detection and intervention in conflicts before they escalate. This may include regular monitoring of conflict indicators such as increased tension or decreased productivity, and proactive measures to address underlying issues before they become more serious.

5. *Diverse conflict resolution options.* Offering a range of conflict resolution options to accommodate the diverse needs and preferences of employees. This includes informal approaches such as coaching or facilitated dialogue, as well as formal processes such as mediation or arbitration. Providing flexibility in conflict resolution mechanisms allows parties to choose the most appropriate approach for their situation.

6. *Collaborative problem-solving.* Promoting a collaborative approach to conflict resolution, where parties work together to identify underlying interests, explore potential solutions, and reach mutually acceptable agreements. This may involve the use of techniques such as negotiation, mediation, or facilitated dialogue to help parties find common ground and resolve their differences.

7. *Feedback and evaluation.* Establishing processes for collecting feedback from employees about their experiences with the conflict management system and using this feedback to make improvements. Regular evaluation of the effectiveness of the conflict strategy ensures that it remains responsive to the evolving needs of the organization.

8. *Integration with organizational culture.* Embedding conflict management principles and practices into the organizational culture to ensure that they are consistently applied and supported throughout the organization. This

involves aligning conflict management with core values, leadership behaviors, and decision-making processes.

9. *Performance management integration.* Integrating conflict resolution principles into performance management processes to address conflicts that may arise in the context of work performance. This includes providing feedback and coaching to employees on conflict-related behaviors and incorporating conflict resolution competencies into performance evaluations.

By bringing together these components within a unified strategy, organizations can effectively manage conflicts, reducing their adverse effects while cultivating a work environment that is both constructive and harmonious. This systematic approach not only aids in the facilitation of communication, collaboration, and trust among employees but also plays a pivotal role in fortifying the organization's resilience and paving the way for its success.

Required Partnerships

When delving into the idea of creating partnerships, it's important to keep in mind what partnership means:

- *Collaborator.* A partner is someone who shares or is involved with another in a particular action or endeavor.

- *Ally.* They are seen as an ally, someone who stands by another's side.

- *Common interest.* Partners are united or associated with others in a shared activity or sphere of common interest.

HR professionals strive to embody these partnership qualities daily, particularly when navigating conflicts. Equipped with an array of tools and strategies, HR professionals are adept at fostering collaboration and synergy within organizations, even under challenging circumstances. Great HR professionals work to break down stovepipes and competitive behaviors among other organizations.

The concept of competitiveness presents an intriguing conundrum, meriting contemplation within the context of conflict resolution. While competitiveness can serve as a catalyst for growth, propelling individuals and teams to strive for excellence, it also harbors the potential for undesirable outcomes. It's a double-edged sword: on one edge lies the impetus for advancement, while on the other lurk behaviors detrimental to workplace harmony.

The "conflict partner scan" underscores the significance of deliberately cultivating specific partnerships to enhance HR's effectiveness in conflict resolution. This proactive approach involves identifying and nurturing various collaborative relationships, each serving a distinct purpose in bolstering HR's support for organizational stakeholders. By fostering these partnerships intentionally, HR can effectively fulfill its role as a reliable resource for conflict resolution and organizational harmony.

HR endeavors to optimize its workforce strategy by forging strategic partnerships across various levels and facets of the organization, particularly in the realm of conflict resolution. Working across boundaries also pays dividends by providing consistent messaging or knowledge transfer as employees work in various realms of the organization. Collaborating with customers and stakeholders ensures that conflict resolution efforts are aligned with organizational goals and priorities. By soliciting feedback and involving customers and stakeholders in conflict resolution processes, HR enhances transparency and accountability. Here's an expanded view of the partnership potentials:

- *Other HR-adjacent specialists within the organization.* Collaborating with fellow HR professionals or colleagues within the organization by working closely with colleagues who specialize in various HR areas such as training, psychology, employee relations, and legal matters, you can share insights, exchange best practices, and offer mutual support in dealing with conflicts.

- *Supervisors.* Building a strong partnership with supervisors enables HR to provide guidance and support in managing conflicts within their teams. By working closely with supervisors, HR can ensure consistent application of conflict resolution strategies and promote a healthy work environment.

- *Senior management.* Aligning with senior management is essential for HR to gain buy-in for conflict resolution initiatives and secure resources necessary for their implementation. Senior management support also lends credibility to HR's efforts in fostering a culture of constructive conflict resolution.

- *Subordinates.* Establishing partnerships with subordinates involves creating open channels of communication and trust, allowing HR to address conflicts from the grassroots level. By soliciting feedback and involving all employees in conflict resolution processes, HR can promote employee engagement and empowerment.

- *Project members.* Collaborating with project teams enables HR to address conflicts that may arise during project execution. By providing conflict resolution support tailored to project dynamics, HR contributes to project success and fosters a culture of collaboration. By offering training and resources on conflict management techniques, HR equips teams with the tools they need to navigate conflicts constructively and achieve innovation goals.

- *Internal peer leaders.* Engaging with internal peer leaders, such as department heads or team leads, allows HR to leverage their influence in resolving conflicts within their respective areas. Building strong partnerships with internal peer leaders facilitates alignment and coordination in conflict resolution efforts.

- *External peer leaders.* External peer leaders, such as counterparts in partner organizations or industry associations, offer valuable perspectives and insights on conflict resolution best practices. Collaborating with external peer leaders broadens HR's knowledge base and enriches its approach to conflict resolution.

- *Process.* Working collaboratively with stakeholders to refine conflict resolution processes ensures that they are effective, efficient, and tailored to organizational needs. By involving key stakeholders in process design and improvement efforts, HR enhances stakeholder buy-in and promotes continuous improvement. Cultivating partnerships focused on enhancing brainstorming skills enables HR to facilitate creative problem-solving and innovation in conflict resolution. By fostering a culture of open dialogue and idea generation, HR empowers employees to explore novel solutions to conflicts.

- *Support staff.* Engaging with support staff, such as budget, HR, legal, and policy teams, allows HR to address conflicts comprehensively and in compliance with organizational policies and regulations. By leveraging expertise from supporting staff, HR ensures that conflict resolution efforts are effective and legally sound.

By integrating key partnership strategies into a robust human capital strategy focused on conflict management, organizations can adeptly navigate conflicts, cultivate a harmonious work environment, and unleash the full potential of their workforce. Prioritizing investments in conflict resolution capabilities not only boosts employee satisfaction and engagement but also plays a pivotal role in driving organizations' success and fortifying resilience. This strategic approach not only fosters a culture of collaboration and open communication but also empowers employees to resolve conflicts constructively, leading to increased productivity, innovation, and overall performance. Embracing conflict as an opportunity for growth and learning enables organizations to build stronger relationships, foster creativity, and adapt more effectively to change, ultimately positioning them for sustained success in today's dynamic business landscape.

A Conflict Resolution Strategic Plan

Picture a company that's all about tackling conflicts strategically. They understand that most of the time, conflicts aren't just one-off problems; they're part of a bigger system. This bigger system resolves interpersonal conflict early and at the lowest level. This bigger system understands the value of rigorous debate of diverse ideas. These companies understand that they must prepare their employees with serious skill-building.

We recommend HR take a step back for a strategy day. Looking strategically at data that only HR and the most senior leadership has access to is a good first step to taking a strategic position. What are the grievances and EEO submissions telling you about conflict? What do your climate surveys and leadership development 360 comments say about conflict? Look at performance improvement plans with an eye toward hidden messages about interpersonal interactions. Are your leadership development classes focused on building conflict resolution skill beyond efforts to say they must step up? This is where Florence, in our opening anecdote, went wrong. Florence was good at the tactical work, but failed to notice the big picture. She didn't look at relevant data, and, moreover, a partnership with the finance department might have at least allowed her to have a heads up about the problem before it was taken to Shannon.

Instead of just telling leaders to step up to conflict and leaving it at that, HR should ensure that the training is giving them solid conflict resolution skills with role-play practice to help them gain confidence. There should be linkage between what you are teaching new employees and what your senior leaders are learning. Keeping this connection between what everyone's learning strong and consistent lowers the chances of people constantly ending up in HR's office with issues.

Writing a strategic plan for conflict resolution does not have to be overly complicated or very different than any strategy you might write. To ensure conflicts in your organization get addressed effectively and proactively, here's a structured approach:

Assess the current situation:

1. Identify existing conflicts within the organization.

2. What motivated you to develop this strategic plan? What were the key ideas or thoughts guiding your decision-making process?

3. Analyze the typical root causes and underlying dynamics of these conflicts.

4. Assess the impact of conflicts on productivity, morale, and organizational culture.

5. Determine the effectiveness of current conflict resolution mechanisms and practices.

Establish clear objectives:

1. Define specific and measurable goals for conflict resolution.

2. Consider both short-term and long-term objectives.

3. Ensure that objectives align with the organization's mission, values, and strategic priorities.

4. Ensure that the objectives align with your motivation for developing the plan.

Develop strategies and tactics:

1. Identify strategies for preventing conflicts before they escalate.

2. Develop tactics for addressing conflicts when they arise, considering the general root causes you identified in the assessment.

3. How will you use alternative dispute resolution methods, such as mediation and conflict coaching, in addition to employee relations approaches you already use?

4. Determine the roles and responsibilities of different organizational specialists in implementing conflict resolution strategies.

Allocate resources:

1. Identify the resources (financial, human, and technological) required to implement the conflict resolution plan effectively.

2. Allocate budget and staffing levels accordingly.

3. Consider training and development needs for employees and managers involved in conflict resolution.

Create communication and reporting mechanisms:

1. Establish clear communication channels for reporting conflicts and seeking assistance.

2. Develop protocols for confidentiality and privacy in conflict resolution processes.

3. Ensure transparency, consistency, and accountability in the handling of conflicts.

4. Implement regular reporting mechanisms to track progress toward conflict resolution goals and adjust strategies as needed.

Promote a culture of conflict resolution:

1. Foster open dialogue and constructive feedback within the organization.

2. Encourage proactive problem-solving and conflict management skills among employees and managers.

3. Recognize and reward positive behaviors related to conflict resolution.

4. Provide training and development opportunities to enhance conflict resolution competencies across the organization.

Monitor and evaluate:

1. Establish key performance indicators to measure the effectiveness of conflict resolution efforts.

2. Conduct regular evaluations to assess the impact of the strategic plan on reducing conflicts and improving organizational dynamics. Will you monitor climate surveys, grievance numbers, or data? Establish and document a baseline in the plan.

3. How will you solicit feedback from employees, managers, and other stakeholders to identify areas of improvement and follow-on data to measure?

4. Use date and feedback to make informed adjustments to the conflict resolution plan as necessary. What will be your time frames for periodic measuring?

By following these steps and incorporating input from relevant stakeholders, you can develop a strategic plan for conflict resolution that addresses the unique needs and challenges of your organization.

While HR writes the plan, when evaluating the implementation of a strategic plan for conflict resolution, it's essential to involve individuals with diverse perspectives and expertise. In large organizations, here's a suggested list of stakeholders who should be in the room. In smaller organizations, bring in in-house experts who will speak to each area:

- *Key decision-makers.* Executives or senior management who have the authority to approve and implement the strategic plan.

- *Conflict resolution specialists.* Experts in conflict resolution methodologies, such as mediators or arbitrators, who can provide insights into best practices and potential challenges.

- *Front-line HR professionals.* HR personnel can offer insights into organizational dynamics, employee concerns, and potential legal implications of the proposed strategies.

- *Legal advisors.* Legal experts can assess the plan's compliance with relevant laws and regulations, as well as potential risks associated with different approaches.

- *Communication specialists.* Professionals with expertise in communication and stakeholder engagement can help ensure that the strategic plan is effectively communicated to all parties involved.

- *Diversity and inclusion representatives.* In conflicts involving issues of diversity, equity, and inclusion, it's important to include representatives who can advocate for marginalized groups and ensure that their perspectives are considered.

- *Ethics and compliance officers.* Professionals responsible for ensuring ethical conduct and compliance with organizational policies can help evaluate the plan's alignment with ethical principles and standards.

Here is an HR pro tip: keep an eye out for opportunities to advocate for conflict resolution. One such opportunity is the annual Conflict Resolution Day, usually observed on the third Thursday of October each year. This day is globally recognized for its focus on promoting peaceful conflict resolution and encouraging individuals to explore the advantages of resolving disputes through nonviolent means. By incorporating Conflict Resolution Day into your strategic plan, you can creatively raise awareness and reaffirm your organization's dedication to proactive conflict resolution.

Fostering allies through a human capital strategy is key to managing conflicts effectively in any organization. By valuing our people and promoting collaboration and empathy, we empower our teams to handle conflicts positively. Building allies strengthens our workplace culture and makes our teams more resilient. Let's keep focusing on developing our human capital to create a culture of teamwork, understanding, and success in conflict management.

Critical Thinking Questions

1. In what ways does a conflict strategic plan contribute to fostering a positive workplace culture and employee satisfaction?

2. What other components to the plan outline discussed in this chapter would you add, and why?

3. How will you as the HR professional ensure that the conflict strategic plan remains agile and adaptable to evolving organizational needs and changes in the external environment?

4. What ethical considerations should be taken into account when developing and implementing a conflict strategic plan, particularly regarding fairness, equity, and transparency in conflict resolution processes?

Dealing with Entrenched Conflict Behaviors

John is at his wits end. Despite his years in HR, he can't crack the code on how to deal with high-performing troublemakers. Today he is meeting with Tanya, who is struggling with a real headache of an employee. This person seems to be actively working against Tanya, using their smarts to cause chaos. Tanya has tried everything—being inviting, collaborating—but nothing works. Now it seems like the only option left is discipline. John worries this employee might quit before facing consequences. He can't help but wonder why some people seem dead set on causing trouble, even though he knows dwelling on it isn't helpful. When Tanya shows up she looks defeated, saying she has nothing left to give. It's either this guy or her, and she knows her worth in the company. She says, "It's him or me, and if I go, good luck because a lot of employees think I'm pretty competent and they are sick of coming to work in this turmoil."

Let's keep it real: sometimes, no matter what we do, there are folks on the team who just seem stuck in a negative mindset. They'd rather stir up trouble than work together, and they thrive on being competitive in all the wrong ways. Some of them aren't shy about their resistance to change, and that can be frustrating. But hey, we also recognize that having a few nonconformists can actually be a good thing—it helps us avoid falling into the trap of groupthink. Then there are those troublemakers who go behind our backs, trying to get others on their side. It's not easy dealing with them, but let's face it, when they come to our attention, we've got to handle it.

HR TIP: When entrenched conflict behaviors are present, take a step back to determine whether invitation mediation or other informal conflict coaching techniques are appropriate first steps. Don't jump in too fast!

We are talking about entrenched conflict behaviors. Entrenched conflict behaviors in employees are deeply ingrained patterns of behavior that stem from unsolved conflicts and breakdowns in communication. These behaviors include blaming others, becoming defensive, escalating hostility, avoiding confrontation, engaging in power struggles, exhibiting bias or stereotypes, and maintaining rigid positions on issues. Resolving such behaviors involves clear communication with the employee, providing direct feedback about unacceptable behavior, setting expectations for change, and holding both the employee and supervisor accountable for actions discussed in meetings with HR. HR might begin to use the term "high-performing troublemaker" out of frustration when other strategies and interventions used don't seem to create progress. In other words, we don't start out referring to our employees as high-performing troublemakers, but instead end up with a term like this after many reasonable conflict resolution options have been tried with no success. While understandable, this resulting mindset about an employee is not helpful.

Discerning the Correct Process

From the get-go, it is important for HR to distinguish the difference between typical conflict behaviors that might become entrenched despite our efforts, as opposed to behaviors that have become so disruptive that mediation and coaching are no longer options. One or both parties in a dispute may display deeply ingrained, adversarial patterns of interaction that are resistant to change. Entrenched conflict sometimes stems from deeply held values and a lack of conflict skills, and it is displayed by verbal outbursts or alliance gathering. Fueled by emotion, an employee may try to save face and be seen as right rather than seek a collaborative solution. This becomes habitual, thus the term "entrenched" is appropriate.

You will begin to suspect you are dealing with an employee with entrenched conflict behaviors when the employee is a repeat customer or is described by others as the root cause of conflict, as is the case in our opening anecdote with Tanya's frustrations.

When you have the thought that "if I could just get these two to see each other's perspective, I think it would help, but yikes this is this going to be a long conversation," then you are likely dealing with an employee with entrenched conflict behaviors. And you're right: conflict skills development and mediation might be great tools to deal with the problem.

As HR professionals, we often find ourselves at the frontline when workplace issues escalate to the point of causing disruption. That's why we've saved this strategy for last—disruption from entrenched conflict behaviors often serves as a catalyst for change, but unnecessary disruption can be subjective. It's up to HR to discern whether these issues warrant disciplinary action or if there's an opportunity to learn and collaborate with leadership to find solutions. Could this disruptive behavior be a sign of deeper underlying issues affecting many employees? What's driving this behavior? As we strive to foster a culture of openness and transparency, HR's role is to approach these questions with curiosity and a commitment to addressing challenges directly.

No matter the complexity or magnitude of the conflict confronting you, there remains an unchanging element at its core—you. Just as you might seek assistance from a skilled computer technician when grappling with challenges beyond your expertise, your leaders are looking to you for direction and insight during turmoil. We urge you to dedicate your full commitment and energy toward resolution before considering punitive measures. Pause to ponder: If the individual is exhibiting entrenched conflict behaviors, what underlying message are they attempting to communicate, and what motives drive their actions? How can you hear their voice more fully?

First Step: Analysis

When you become aware of entrenched conflict behaviors in the workplace, or when a leader describes an employees as "too difficult to deal with," it's important to approach the situation thoughtfully and systematically. As you assess how the disruption affects work, culture, and team dynamics, adopt a neutral perspective. We deliberately refer to all our employees as high performers, assuming that every staff member is capable of excelling in their role. These employees who appear disruptive may actually provide valuable insights into our organizational culture. Are they perceived as difficult because they are—

- *Overconfident.* Sometimes this overconfidence leads them to challenge authority. Sometimes these employees have been so propped up with straight As in school that they can be overly sensitive to any constructive feedback.

- *Desiring more autonomy.* High performers can especially resist working for micromanaging leaders.

- *Competitive.* Are they trying to gain an edge over their colleagues? Why?

- *Frustrated.* Do they feel their contributions are undervalued or is their work taking decades to get implemented?

- *Bored.* We recall a mediation where one employee told the leader they admitted to acting out because they had little work to do that was challenging.

- *Lacking emotional intelligence in general.* Does this employee display poor interpersonal skills in general? Could they benefit from conflict resolution training?

- *Having personal issues.* Like anyone else, your employee may have challenges outside of work that can result in disruptive behavior in the workplace.

The only way to know is through a good intake process with all involved. Once you gain additional insight, when mediating or coaching through conflicts involving entrenched behaviors, it's essential for HR to navigate beyond surface-level positions or generalizations, and delve into the underlying values or interests that may or may not be shared among the parties involved. This process allows for a deeper understanding of each party's perspective and creates opportunities for finding common ground and facilitating meaningful resolutions. By focusing on underlying values, the mediator can help bridge divides and foster mutual respect and understanding among conflicting parties.

Identifying the underlying issues can help you decide next steps. Take note of instances of disruptive behavior and identify any patterns or triggers. What was the context of the disruption? Then have an open and honest conversation with the individual who is being disruptive to learn motivations and concerns. In this conversation, be especially specific, like in this example: "It's come to my attention that [name the behavior]. The impact of that behavior was [name it]. I'm here today to try to understand your point of view, and to gain your agreement to move forward in a more productive manner. Why don't we start by you telling me what's going on from your perspective." End this first session with clear expectations for behavior and performance within the team. Make sure the employee understands the impact of their behavior on others and the consequences of continued disruptions. It is squarely HR's job to address unproductive teaming behaviors that cause business problems.

Next Step: Intervention Strategies

Let's plan out our next steps clearly. First, we need to make sure everyone knows what's expected of them. This means laying out who does what, what their responsibilities are, and what kind of behavior we expect. If anyone needs help meeting these expectations you'll provide support, whether that's extra training, guidance, or resources. It's also important to adhere to productive teaming behaviors and to let everyone know that there are consequences for disruptive behavior. HR professionals know more than most that we do occasionally run across employees who seem determined to be disruptive, but we also know that this is actually rarer than water cooler gossip suggests.

A KEY INTERVENTION PARTNER

Partnering with psychologists can be a valuable approach for addressing entrenched conflict behaviors in the workplace. Here's how such a partnership might work:

- *Conflict analysis and assessment.* Psychologists can conduct thorough assessments to understand the underlying psychological factors contributing to entrenched conflict behaviors. This may involve individual assessments of the parties involved, as well as broader assessments of team dynamics and organizational culture.

- *Intervention strategies.* Based on their expertise in human behavior and psychology, psychologists can develop tailored intervention strategies to address entrenched conflict behaviors. These strategies may include individual counseling or therapy sessions, group therapy, conflict resolution workshops, or team-building exercises designed to improve communication and foster empathy.

- *Skills training.* Psychologists can partner with you to conduct training sessions to equip employees and managers with the skills necessary to effectively manage conflict and navigate challenging interpersonal dynamics. This may include training in communication skills, emotional intelligence, assertiveness, and conflict resolution techniques.

- *Support for HR professionals.* HR professionals may also benefit from psychological support and guidance in managing complex conflict situations. Psychologists can provide consultation and supervision to HR professionals, helping them to navigate challenging cases and develop effective strategies for conflict resolution.

Partnering with psychologists can enhance HR's capacity to address entrenched conflict behaviors in the workplace by providing specialized expertise in human behavior, psychological assessment, intervention strategies, and conflict resolution techniques. By working collaboratively, HR and psychologists can create a supportive and conducive environment for resolving conflicts and fostering positive interpersonal relationships within the organization.

Special Workplace Concerns: Bullying and Mutiny

HR frequently has to address bully behavior in the workplace, but HR should not view it as an entrenched conflict behavior. Bullying is a form of aggressive behavior that involves repeated, intentional harm inflicted upon another individual or group, typically characterized by an imbalance of power. This harm can manifest in various forms, including physical, verbal, emotional, or social abuse. Examples of bullying behaviors may include verbal insults, spreading rumors, exclusion, intimidation, physical aggression, or online harassment. It's important to differentiate bullying from conflict. While conflict involves a disagreement or clash of interests between parties, bullying is characterized by an abuse of power and a deliberate intent to cause harm.[5] Bullying is not considered a conflict behavior because it does not involve a mutual dis-agreement or negotiation between parties. Instead, it is a form of abusive behavior that seeks to exert power and control over others, often with harmful consequences. Bullying requires investigation, discipline, and possibly expert mental health intervention before any attempt at restorative conversations. Still, we have conducted mediations as a way to restore working relationships when both parties want a sit-down, and the bully shows the ability to seek perspective (after considerable inter-vention work). In summary, we would not start by addressing a bully/victim conflict with mediation or conflict coaching.

One particular conflict scenario that also warrants specific discussion when choosing which next step you'll take is when employees attempt to overthrow their leader through covert means, a behavior commonly referred to as mutiny. This kind of behavior can have significant and far-reaching impacts on team performance, morale, and overall effectiveness. When employees engage in attempted mutiny against team leaders or management, it undermines the credibility and authority of

---

5   Megan Morfitt Carle, *Walk Away to Win: A Playbook to Combat Workplace Bullying* (New York: McGraw Hill, 2023).

those in leadership positions. This loss of trust in leadership further escalates the conflict and complicates its resolution. Leaders often remain unaware of this behavior until it has already caused considerable damage.

The repercussions of mutinous behavior extend beyond the internal dynamics of the team, affecting external stakeholders such as clients, partners, or investors. News of internal strife or attempts to overthrow leadership can tarnish the organization's reputation and negatively influence perceptions of the team or organization. This can result in a fractured team, decreased productivity, and low morale, making it challenging for the organization to achieve its goals and remain competitive.

Timely and decisive intervention is essential, particularly when instances of mutiny surface, demanding swift and resolute action. You need to delve into the root causes, addressing them comprehensively, and placing particular emphasis on fostering a renewed sense of trust within the team. Our suggestion entails engaging directly with the implicated employees, ensuring that grievances are aired and conflicts are resolved in a constructive manner. Subsequent steps should involve facilitating team mediation sessions aimed at fostering open dialogue and resolving any lingering tensions, thereby promoting a harmonious and productive work environment.

As HR, the initial step in addressing mutiny upon becoming aware of it is to gather thorough information about the situation. This entails reaching out to all involved parties individually to gain insight into their perspectives and gather pertinent facts.

It's important to create a safe environment for employees to voice their concerns and grievances without fearing repercussions, while also clarifying that consultation with leadership will be necessary. When engaging with stakeholders, particularly senior management and legal counsel in cases involving multiple employees, prioritize discussions on resolution rather than dwelling solely on the causes. Subsequently, develop a plan and assist leadership in its implementation.

A Comprehensive Approach to Entrenched Conflict

HR's role in managing deep-rooted conflict behaviors centers around open communication, empathy, and peaceful resolution. It's about fostering an environment where trust and understanding can thrive. By taking proactive measures, educating all involved parties, and emphasizing respect as a core value, conflicts can be transformed into opportunities for growth and collaboration. While it may seem like addressing conflicts consumes the majority of your time, investing in a comprehensive conflict strategy upfront can ultimately reduce workload later on. HR also needs to develop and implement a holistic strategy for handling conflict, ensuring that individual disputes are addressed within the broader context of organizational goals and values. Ultimately, this comprehensive approach contributes to employee satisfaction and organizational success.

Employees who operate within an environment where their

diverse perspectives are embraced and valued tend to exhibit higher levels of productivity. When individuals feel appreciated for their unique contributions and respected for their viewpoints, they are more inclined to engage fully in their work. This inclusive atmosphere fosters a sense of belonging and camaraderie among team members, reducing the prevalence of entrenched conflict behaviors. As a result, collaboration flourishes, communication becomes more effective, and collective efforts are directed toward achieving shared goals. By nurturing a culture that celebrates diversity and promotes mutual respect, organizations can cultivate a workforce that is not only happier but also more motivated, innovative, and ultimately, more successful. If you find yourself investing significant time addressing entrenched behaviors, it may be beneficial to revisit your conflict strategy and implement adjustments to steer toward a more constructive course of action.

Critical Thinking Questions

1. What biases or assumptions do you bring into conflict resolution process when dealing with entrenched behaviors, and how do they impact your approach?

2. How do you manage your emotions during conflict resolution processes with employees who have entrenched behaviors? Are you calm and composed, or do you become easily agitated or frustrated?

3. How do you prioritize self-care and manage your own stress when dealing with challenging conflict situations on a regular basis?

Parting Thoughts

As we reach the end of this book journey together, we want to take a moment to acknowledge the rollercoaster of emotions, insights, and revelations we've experienced along the way. It's been quite a ride, hasn't it? From the initial frustration and overwhelm to the gradual realization that, perhaps, conflict isn't the enemy we once thought it to be.

Let's be honest—when you first picked up this book some of you might have been feeling a bit burnt out, maybe even a tad cynical. The relentless tide of workplace drama can take its toll, leaving us questioning our sanity and our career choices. But here's the thing—in the chaos, there lies an opportunity. An opportunity to redefine our relationship with conflict, to transform it from a source of stress into a catalyst for positive change.

Think back to why you first entered the field of HR. Was it the allure of problem-solving, the desire to make a difference in people's lives, or perhaps just a deep-seated curiosity about the human condition? Whatever it was, we urge you to reconnect with that sense of purpose, that spark of enthusiasm that brought you here in the first place.

In the wake of the pandemic and as we traverse the world of AI, the need for skilled conflict resolution professionals has never been greater. Leaders and employees alike are looking to us for guidance, for understanding, and for that rare combination of empathy and decisiveness that only HR professionals can provide. It's a daunting task, to be sure, but it's also an incredible opportunity to make a meaningful impact on organizational culture.

Throughout this book we've shared stories, strategies, and insights gleaned from our collective years of experience in the trenches of HR. But more than that, we've shared a vision—a vision of a workplace where conflict is not something to be feared, but embraced; where diversity of thought is celebrated, and constructive dialogue is the norm.

As you close the final pages of *Conflict Sparks Change*, know that you're not alone on this journey. We are a community, bound together by our shared passion for helping others navigate the complexities of human interaction. So let's lean on each other for support, for encouragement, and yes, even for a little bit of humor when things get tough. Fellow practitioners, let's embrace the challenge of conflict transformation with open hearts and open minds. Let's harness the power of controversy to drive positive change, and let's never lose sight of the incredible impact we can have on the organizations we serve.

KIM FAIRCLOTH
DAWN BEDLIVY

Acknowledgments

Writing this book has been an incredible learning experience. We owe a great deal of gratitude to the expert team at Greenleaf Book Group for their invaluable guidance and support. Their publishing proficiency allowed us to focus on our strengths while entrusting them with the crucial task of bringing our work to its final, polished form. We are deeply appreciative of their dedication and expertise in ensuring our book reached its highest potential.

We also want to acknowledge all our mentors who have supported us along the way. While there are many—and you know who you are!—we would like to specifically mention Craig Runde and Terry Marschall, our original ADR mentors. We are also grateful to the Atlanta Justice Center and Mediation Training Institute, our initial sources of mediation training. Additionally, we extend our thanks to the Co-Active Training Institute and the CRR Global's Organization and Relationship Systems Coaching (ORSC) communities for broadening our coaching perspectives and methods beyond what we thought was possible.

Appendix A

Mediator's Process Planner

This planning template will help mediators smoothly navigate mediation sessions, promoting fairness, teamwork, and positive conflict resolution in the workplace. You are encouraged to tweak it to match your own style and methods.

Intake Process	Pre-Mediation Caucus	Joint Session	Closure
1. Establish boundaries on confidentiality guarantees. 2. Clarify business impact. 3. Set expectations with leaders.	1. Ensure there are no underlying issues that might affect the process. Address ongoing legal cases, medical conditions, or job change impacts. 2. Explain the mediation event process to include confidentiality. 3. Address both meeting and scheduling logistics. 4. Discuss behavioral rules of engagement. 5. Encourage participants to consider their objectives and imagine the other parties' goals. 6. Address contingency plans for technology issues. 7. Confirm that a similar meeting will happen or has happened with the other party. 8. Emphasize voluntary participation. 9. Explain your role as a neutral dialogue facilitator.	1. Remind the parties of the business rules of engagement. 2. Encourage voluntary participation to include note-taking rules and that all notes except the outcomes will be destroyed. 3. Begin with uninterrupted opening remarks. 4. Acknowledge progress toward breakthrough. 5. Ask open-ended questions and allow for silence to facilitate reflection. 6. Call participants by preferred name.	1. Navigate impasses by asking a question to parties regarding potential outcomes if agreement seems unattainable. Offer second mediation. 2. Encourage brainstorming of multiple ideas. Use AI when appropriate. 3. Take enduring outcome notes and read each note aloud for joint editing. 4. Thank participants for their commitment and efforts throughout the session. 5. Tell the participants you will type and email one email with the agreed-upon outcomes to both participants. Lead a discussion about how they will jointly present those outcomes to the appropriate organizational leader.

Appendix B

Perspective-Seeking Activity

The purpose of this worksheet is to help you reflect and consider the perspectives of all parties involved in the conflict. By completing the activity, you can gain insights that can contribute to a more constructive and empathetic conflict conversation.

Instructions:

1. For each question, take the time to reflect on the perspective you have and the potential perspective of the other party involved in the conflict.

2. Write down your thoughts and feelings in response to each question. You will not be sharing this activity sheet.

3. Be thoughtful as you consider the other party's point of view. You may or may not know someone else's perspective prior to the discussion, but you can start to be curious.

4. This forward-thinking perspective-seeking activity can provide you greater clarity and contribute to a more effective and mutually beneficial resolution.

Self-contemplation/ awareness	Putting yourself in the shoes of the other party	Areas of agreement and disagreement
1. What are your top three goals or desired outcomes for this conflict discussion? 2. Describe your thoughts, feelings, and concerns regarding this conflict. 3. In what ways do you believe your actions or words may have been perceived by the other party?	1. What do you believe are the key concerns and interests of the other party? What do you think the ideal resolution looks like from the perspective of the other party? 2. How do you think the other party feels about the situation? What emotions might they be experiencing? 3. What do you think led the other party to take the actions that have contributed to the conflict? How do you believe the other party's background, experiences, or values have influenced their perspective on this conflict?	1. What aspects of the conflict do you both seem to agree upon? In what ways will you leverage these areas of agreement to build rapport and facilitate resolution? 2. List what you anticipate will be the harder points of contention or disagreement between you and the other party. Take a minute to try to understand the underlying reasons or motivations behind these differences. 3. How can you express your own needs and concerns while also actively listening to and validating the other party's perspective? How do you want to be remembered after this discussion is over?

About the Authors

Kim Faircloth (PhD, SHRM-SCP, SPHR) is a seasoned professional with over 30 years of experience in conflict resolution coaching and mediation, leadership development, and executive coaching. As the co-owner of Conflict Sparks Change, LLC, she empowers individuals and organizations to effectively manage conflicts and enhance employee engagement. A certified coach and trained mediator, Dr. Faircloth has guided thousands in addressing workplace conflicts. Her expertise spans roles such as ombudsman, workforce strategies consultant, and director of human resources. Drawing on her doctoral studies in conflict and mediation, she is a senior principal trainer and consultant at the Mediation Training Institute based in St. Petersburg, Florida. She continues to make significant contributions to the field, driven by her commitment to peacemaking and educating future HR professionals.

Dawn Bedlivy (Esq) is a distinguished conflict resolution specialist with over three decades of experience. Her expertise encompasses leadership development, alternative dispute resolution, and conflict systems design. Ms. Bedlivy has successfully led teams and delivered consultation and training at prestigious venues. As an accomplished ombudsman, mediator, and organizational systems coach, she has applied her skills to spearhead an innovation ecosystem. Demonstrating her commitment to education, Ms. Bedlivy serves as adjunct faculty at the University of Maryland Francis King Carey School of Law, where she educates future professionals in conflict resolution.